Institutional Research in Transition

Marvin W. Peterson, Mary Corcoran, *Editors*

NEW DIRECTIONS FOR INSTITUTIONAL RESEARCH
Sponsored by the Association for Institutional Research
PATRICK T. TERENZINI, *Editor-in-Chief*
MARVIN W. PETERSON, *Associate Editor*

Number 46, June 1985

Paperback sourcebooks in
The Jossey-Bass Higher Education Series

Jossey-Bass Inc., Publishers
San Francisco • Washington • London

378
.155
N532
1985
no.46 AUG 2 5 1995

Marvin W. Peterson, Mary Corcoran, (Eds.).
Institutional Research in Transition.
New Directions for Institutional Research, no. 46.
Volume XII, number 2.
San Francisco: Jossey-Bass, 1985

New Directions for Institutional Research Series
Patrick T. Terenzini, *Editor-in-Chief*
Marvin W. Peterson, *Associate Editor*

Copyright © 1985 by Jossey-Bass Inc., Publishers
  and
  Jossey-Bass Limited

Copyright under International, Pan American, and Universal Copyright Conventions. All rights reserved. No part of this issue may be reproduced in any form — except for brief quotation (not to exceed 500 words) in a review or professional work — without permission in writing from the publishers.

New Directions for Institutional Research (publication number USPS 098-830) is published quarterly by Jossey-Bass Inc., Publishers, and is sponsored by the Association for Institutional Research. The volume and issue numbers above are included for the convenience of libraries. Second-class postage rates paid at San Francisco, California, and at additional mailing offices.

Correspondence:
Subscriptions, single-issue orders, change of address notices, undelivered copies, and other correspondence should be sent to Subscriptions, Jossey-Bass Inc., Publishers, 433 California Street, San Francisco, California 94104.

Editorial correspondence should be sent to the Editor-in-Chief, Patrick Terenzini; Office of Institutional Research, SUNY, Albany, New York 12222, or Associate Editor, Marvin W. Peterson, Center for the Study of Higher Education, University of Michigan, Ann Arbor, Michigan 48109.

Library of Congress Catalogue Card Number LC 84-82373

International Standard Serial Number ISSN 0271-0579

International Standard Book Number ISBN 87589-752-5

Cover art by Willi Baum
Manufactured in the United States of America

Ordering Information

The paperback sourcebooks listed below are published quarterly and can be ordered either by subscription or single-copy.

Subscriptions cost $35.00 per year for institutions, agencies, and libraries. Individuals can subscribe at the special rate of $25.00 per year *if payment is by personal check*. (Note that the full rate of $35.00 applies if payment is by institutional check, even if the subscription is designated for an individual.) Standing orders are accepted. Subscriptions normally begin with the first of the four sourcebooks in the current publication year of the series. When ordering, please indicate if you prefer your subscription to begin with the first issue of the *coming* year.

Single copies are available at $8.95 when payment accompanies order, and *all single-copy orders under $25.00 must include payment*. (California, New Jersey, New York, and Washington, D.C., residents please include appropriate sales tax.) For billed orders, cost per copy is $8.95 plus postage and handling. (Prices subject to change without notice.)

Bulk orders (ten or more copies) of any individual sourcebook are available at the following discounted prices: 10–49 copies, $8.05 each; 50–100 copies, $7.15 each; over 100 copies, *inquire*. Sales tax and postage and handling charges apply as for single copy orders.

To ensure correct and prompt delivery, all orders must give either the *name of an individual* or an *official purchase order number*. Please submit your order as follows:

Subscriptions: specify series and year subscription is to begin.
Single Copies: specify sourcebook code (such as, IR8) and first two words of title.

Mail orders for United States and Possessions, Latin America, Canada, Japan, Australia, and New Zealand to:
Jossey-Bass Inc., Publishers
433 California Street
San Francisco, California 94104

Mail orders for all other parts of the world to:
Jossey-Bass Limited
28 Banner Street
London EC1Y 8QE

New Directions for Institutional Research Series
Patrick T. Terenzini, *Editor-in-Chief*
Marvin W. Peterson, *Associate Editor*

IR1 *Evaluating Institutions for Accountability,* Howard R. Bowen
IR2 *Assessing Faculty Effort,* James I. Doi
IR3 *Toward Affirmative Action,* Lucy W. Sells

IR4   *Organizing Nontraditional Study,* Samuel Baskin
IR5   *Evaluating Statewide Boards,* Robert O. Berdahl
IR6   *Assuring Academic Progress Without Growth,* Allan M. Cartter
IR7   *Responding to Changing Human Resource Needs,* Paul Heist, Jonathan R. Warren
IR8   *Measuring and Increasing Academic Productivity,* Robert A. Wallhaus
IR9   *Assessing Computer-Based System Models,* Thomas R. Mason
IR10 *Examining Departmental Management,* James Smart, James Montgomery
IR11 *Allocating Resources Among Departments,* Paul L. Dressel,
      Lou Anna Kimsey Simon
IR12 *Benefiting from Interinstitutional Research,* Marvin W. Peterson
IR13 *Applying Analytic Methods to Planning and Management,* David S. P. Hopkins,
      Roger G. Schroeder
IR14 *Protecting Individual Rights to Privacy in Higher Education,* Alton L. Taylor
IR15 *Appraising Information Needs of Decision Makers,* Carl R. Adams
IR16 *Increasing the Public Accountability of Higher Education,* John K. Folger
IR17 *Analyzing and Constructing Cost,* Meredith A. Gonyea
IR18 *Employing Part-Time Faculty,* David W. Leslie
IR19 *Using Goals in Research and Planning,* Robert Fenske
IR20 *Evaluating Faculty Performance and Vitality,* Wayne C. Kirschling
IR21 *Developing a Total Marketing Plan,* John A. Lucas
IR22 *Examining New Trends in Administrative Computing,* E. Michael Staman
IR23 *Professional Development for Institutional Research,* Robert G. Cope
IR24 *Planning Rational Retrenchment,* Alfred L. Cooke
IR25 *The Impact of Student Financial Aid on Institutions,* Joe B. Henry
IR26 *The Autonomy of Public Colleges,* Paul L. Dressel
IR27 *Academic Program Evaluation,* Eugene C. Craven
IR28 *Academic Planning for the 1980s,* Richard B. Heydinger
IR29 *Institutional Assessment for Self-Improvement,* Richard I. Miller
IR30 *Coping with Faculty Reduction,* Stephen R. Hample
IR31 *Evaluation of Management and Planning Systems,* Nick L. Poulton
IR32 *Increasing the Use of Program Evaluation,* Jack Lindquist
IR33 *Effective Planned Change Strategies,* G. Melvin Hipps
IR34 *Qualitative Methods for Institutional Research,* Eileen Kuhns, S. V. Martorana
IR35 *Information Technology: Advances and Applications,* Bernard Sheehan
IR36 *Studying Student Attrition,* Ernest T. Pascarella
IR37 *Using Research for Strategic Planning,* Norman P. Uhl
IR38 *The Politics and Pragmatics of Institutional Research,* James W. Firnberg,
      William F. Lasher
IR39 *Applying Methods and Techniques of Futures Research,* James L. Morrison,
      William L. Renfro, Wayne I. Boucher
IR40 *College Faculty: Versatile Human Resources in a Period of Constraint,*
      Roger G. Baldwin, Robert T. Blackburn
IR41 *Determining the Effectiveness of Campus Services,* Robert A. Scott
IR42 *Issues in Pricing Undergraduate Education,* Larry H. Litten
IR43 *Responding to New Realities in Funding,* Larry L. Leslie
IR44 *Using Microcomputers for Planning and Management Support,* William L. Tetlow
IR45 *Impact and Challenges of a Changing Federal Role,* Virginia Ann Hodgkinson

Contents

Editors' Notes 1
Marvin W. Peterson, Mary Corcoran

Chapter 1. Institutional Research: An Evolutionary Perspective 5
Marvin W. Peterson
The practice and profession of institutional research and the Association for Institutional Research, which emerged in the 1950s and which grew and consolidated in the 1970s in response to the changing concerns of higher education, face fragmentation and uncertainty in the 1980s.

Chapter 2. The Art and Science of Institutional Research 17
Cameron Fincher
Institutional research is a practicing art. Its merits lie in its relevance to and its influence on decision and policy making. A more positive attitude toward theory-related research would enhance its future development.

Chapter 3. Forces Affecting the Future of Postsecondary Education 39
Richard B. Heydinger
Changes in the external environment will have an increasing impact on colleges and universities. Institutional researchers must develop broad integrative skills to monitor these changes.

Chapter 4. Changing Governance and Management Strategies 59
Frank Schmidtlein
External changes and new technological developments combine with new perspectives on organizations to change institutional governance and management in ways that challenge some conventions of institutional research practice.

Chapter 5. Telematics and the Decision Support Intermediary 81
Bernard S. Sheehan
Advanced communication and computing technologies create new resources and new opportunities in expanded role relationships for institutional research.

Chapter 6. Proliferation or Professional Integration: Transition or Transformation 99
Marvin W. Peterson, Mary Corcoran
The implications of the new environmental realities of postsecondary education governance and management and telematics for institutional research as a practice and profession challenge the Association for Institutional Research to take a more proactive transformational leadership strategy for the development of the profession.

Index 113

The Association for Institutional Research was created in 1966 to benefit, assist, and advance research leading to improved understanding, planning, and operation of institutions of higher education. Publication policy is set by its Publications Board.

PUBLICATIONS BOARD
Stephen R. Hample (Chairperson), Montana State University
Ellen E. Chaffee, National Center for Higher Education Management Systems
Jean J. Endo, University of Colorado at Boulder
Cameron L. Fincher, University of Georgia
Richard B. Heydinger, University of Minnesota
Penny A. Wallhaus, Illinois Community College Board

EX-OFFICIO MEMBERS OF THE PUBLICATIONS BOARD
Charles F. Elton, University of Kentucky
Elizabeth F. Fox, University of Alabama in Birmingham
Gerald W. McLaughlin, Virginia Polytechnic Institute & State University
Marvin W. Peterson, University of Michigan
Patrick T. Terenzini, State University of New York at Albany

EDITORIAL ADVISORY BOARD
All members of the Publications Board and:
Frederick E. Balderston, University of California, Berkeley
Howard R. Bowen, Claremont Graduate School
Roberta D. Brown, Arkansas College
Lyman A. Glenny, University of California, Berkeley (retired)
David S. P. Hopkins, Stanford University
Roger G. Schroeder, University of Minnesota
Robert J. Silverman, Ohio State University
Martin A. Trow, University of California, Berkeley

For information about the Association for Institutional Research, write:

    AIR Executive Office
    314 Stone Building
    Florida State University
    Tallahassee, FL 32306

    (904)644-4470

Editors' Notes

This volume of *New Directions for Institutional Research* coincides with the twenty-fifth annual forum of the Association of Institutional Research (AIR). It is neither designed nor intended to be a thorough history of the practice of institutional research or of AIR itself. Nor is it intended to examine the many ongoing, important functions or responsibilities that have typically become associated with institutional research on many campuses, such as data base development and management, reporting to agencies and responding to external data requests, and conducting the many important, regular analyses and studies done to inform planning, resource allocation, evaluation, and other management and decision-making activities in all areas of the institution. Most of these functions have been well documented at AIR annual forums and in various publications, and most will continue.

The intent is to use the occasion of the twenty-fifth forum to be both retrospective and prospective—but primarily prospective. Our view is that institutional research has succeeded in large measure because it has historically been on the cutting edge of new and emerging challenges to institutions of higher education and because it has helped them to adapt to those challenges. This volume addresses the broad issues and forces affecting the function and direction of institutional research, not the ongoing activities.

The volume has four primary purposes: to examine the development of the field, assess its stage of development, and determine the patterns that have led to its success (Chapter One); to assess the current theoretical and methodological state of the field and its contributions (Chapter Two); to examine three major, rapidly changing environmental forces—education, governance, and telematics—that have significant implications for institutional research (Chapters Three, Four, and Five); and to define the major challenges that may reshape the future patterns both of practice and of professional development in institutional research (Chapter Six).

Our overriding purpose is to define the major challenges that may reshape the patterns both of practice and of professional development in the field as we look to the future. Institutional research must continue to develop in a manner which ensures that it makes a major, positive contribution to improvements in the quality and performance of our institutions of higher education.

A Framework

Two analytic perspectives are implicit in this volume. First, we see institutional research as an institutional function or activity in the middle—an intermediary function that links the educational, governance, and information

1

functions of institutions of higher education. This perspective enlarges on previous conceptions of institutional research.

The concern of institutional researchers for the educational enterprise—for describing and assessing students, faculty, resources, curricula, programs, and research—has been well understood since institutional research began. The relationship of institutional research to the governance and management structure and the concern for providing useful decision support information and research have been long-standing concerns. The role and interests of institutional research in information system development and in data exchange and utilization have become well established in the past decade. Institutional research has in fact been described as the intermediary function between requesters and suppliers of data. However, the relationship between the larger external environments of our institutions' educational, governance, and information functions and the institutional research functions has not received careful attention. That analytic perspective informs Chapters Three, Four, and Five, which scrutinize changes in the external environment and suggest their implications for institutional research.

Second, our analytic perspective characterizes institutional research as a field of practice, a profession, and an association. The term *practice* is used to connote both the way in which day-to-day institutional research activities are organized (function and structure) and the things that are done in institutional settings (type of studies, methods, concern for information system). The term *profession* refers to characteristics of institutional researchers as representatives of a more or less clearly defined professional group (their professional nature and primary common concerns) and their common individual characteristics (identification with, motivations toward, and preparation for the profession). It also includes the conceptual or theoretical and methodological sophistication of the profession and its standards of practice. The term *association* refers to the organizational entity that represents the profession (the AIR) in terms of its major focus, primary function, and major initiatives. This framework is used in Chapter One to examine the development of institutional research and understand some reasons for its success. Chapter Two focuses on the conceptual and methodological character of the art and science of institutional research and on its standards and norms. Chapter Six returns to our concern for institutional research as practice, profession, and association.

An Overview

In Chapter One, Marvin Peterson draws on his extensive experience in the study of higher education, including institutional research, and on his involvement in the AIR to describe key developments over the past two-and-one-half decades of institutional research as practice, profession, and association. This perspective reflects the development of institutional research during a period that coincides with a growing interest in the management of colleges and universities. As a field, institutional research has grown and expanded by focusing on challenges and problems affecting higher education and by constantly adapting to those challenges. Peterson concludes by suggesting that many of today's assumptions and uncertainties about the role and direction of institutional research may be compounded by changes in three important environments for institutional research—education, governance, and telematics.

In Chapter Two, Cameron Fincher applies his scholarly interest in the field of institutional research to assess the current state of the art and science of the profession, its theory and its methodology. He summarizes both the extensive contributions and the shortcomings of institutional research when it is viewed as an integrated professional field.

Chapters Three, Four, and Five examine developments in the environment and their implications for institutional research. In Chapter Three, Richard Heydinger uses his interest in environmental scanning and institutional planning to examine the demands of the changing educational environment that may be reshaping our postsecondary system and institutions and suggests strategic implications for institutional research. He asks what the new concerns of institutional research must be if institutional research is to serve the changing educational role and function of our institutions. In Chapter Four, Frank Schmidtlein uses his administrative experience with and scholarly knowledge of governance and management research and practice in postsecondary institutions to examine the changing managerial and governance issues and strategies that are reshaping the decision processes of our systems and institutions. He asks how these changes will affect the decision makers, the decision-making process, and the concern for analysis and research. In Chapter Five, Bernard Sheehan combines his extensive institutional and professional experience in the field with his scholarly interest in management sciences to examine the changing developments in information and telecommunications technology that are reshaping the analytic and management decision practices in higher education. He asks how these developments will change the analytic role of decision making and our institutional processes for information design, analysis, and decision support. All three chapters suggest implications for the content, process, and structure of institutional research.

In Chapter Six, Marvin Peterson and Mary Corcoran assess the implications of these three environmental forces for institutional research. They identify some of the dilemmas that these forces pose for the field and for practice, and they ask some questions that the profession must address if institutional research is to adapt to these challenges and continue to play an important role in the planning, management, allocation, and evaluation functions of our institutions of postsecondary education. One critical question is whether the transitional strategy of responding and adapting to institutional and environmental changes that now prevails in the profession and the association is sufficient for a future that threatens to fragment the field and emerging profession. A transformational strategy, whereby the association actively attempts to guide and direct the development of the profession, may be necessary to ensure that it continues to make a valuable contribution to the continuing improvement of postsecondary education.

Marvin W. Peterson
Mary Corcoran
Editors

Marvin W. Peterson is director of the Center for the Study of Higher Education at the University of Michigan. He is now president of the Association for Institutional Research.

Mary Corcoran is professor of higher education and educational psychology at the University of Minnesota. She is a former editor of AIR forum publications, and a Distinguished Member of the Association.

The growth and development of the practice, the profession, and the Association of Institutional Research have been closely intertwined. They have both responded to and been affected by conditions affecting institutions of higher education.

Institutional Research: An Evolutionary Perspective

Marvin W. Peterson

Although the field of institutional research did not begin with the first AIR forum, it has grown remarkably in the past two-and-one-half decades, beginning with the now notorious invitational gathering of forty-six concerned individuals in Chicago in 1961. While those who attended that forum were accurate in anticipating the need for data and research to improve institutions of higher learning (Brumbaugh, 1960), few could have anticipated the growth, expansion, and professional development that characterized the field during the following years. However, the intent of this chapter is not to recount the history of these twenty-five years in any detail but to provide some useful historical or retrospective examination. (For a history of institutional research prior to 1961, see Cowley, 1959; for an early account of the formal beginning of the field, see Doi, 1979).

The primary contention of this chapter is that institutional research is at a very critical stage in its development. In the midst of the third decade of organized institutional research, it is a critical intermediary function that links the educational, managerial, and information functions of higher education institutions and systems. While institutional research has always been linked to these three functions, it has tended at any one time to be primarily identified with only one of the three as institutions have focused their concerns on that area. In the late 1960s, the dominant issue was governance. In the early and mid 1970s, information systems came to the fore, and in the late 1970s, educational issues were primary. The major question was always one of how to improve the particular area during a period of relative institutional growth or stability. In such a context, institutional research has responded well and helped to meet institutional needs while expanding its own repertory of concepts, methods, and skills.

In the mid 1980s, conditions facing the field of institutional research are both quantitatively and qualitatively different. Most institutions are suffering enrollment declines and financial constraints, not growth or stability. Institutions must face extensive and substantial challenges simultaneously in their educational, governance, and information system environments. These changes place critical demands on or have significant implications for the nature of our institutions and for the shape and practice of institutional research. At recent AIR forums, some members have asked whether institutional research can continue to adapt, whether it will become a set of subsidiary activities allocated to other administrative offices, whether it will become a routine technical function, or whether it is subject to Peterson's organizational corollary of the so-called Peter principle — an organizational activity that has risen to its level of incompetence (Peterson, 1971).

An Evolutionary Overview: Practice, Profession, and Association

Characterizing an entire field on three broad dimensions in a single, short chapter can only be done in a very general way. However, the intent is to portray the evolution of the field so as to obtain some insight into why it has evolved as it has and to see what can be learned that can guide us in responding to the new challenges posed by changing educational, governance, and telematics environments. This section reflects the author's synthesis of the literature of institutional research, his knowledge of past forums and AIR publications, and his personal experience with the AIR. For the purposes of discussion, it is useful to review the organized era of institutional research in three phases or stages (Peterson, 1979; also see Table 1).

The Emergence of Institutional Research: The 1950s and 1960s. Although there were historical precursors (Cowley, 1959), the formally organized practice of institutional research emerged in the 1950s and expanded rapidly in the 1960s (Doi, 1979). During this era, institutions of higher education struggled with issues raised by growing enrollments, expanding campuses, and an increasingly complex array of curricular offerings and administrative structures. Executive officers were concerned about obtaining data and information that could guide the advancement of robust institutions. Presidential concern about the absence of data and the need for institutional research is reflected in the decision of the American Council on Education (ACE) in 1957 to establish an office of statistical information and research.

Table 1. The Evolution of Institutional Research: Practice, Profession, and Association

	1950s and 1960s: Emergence of Institutional Research	1970s: Growth and Consolidation	1980s: Fragmentation and Uncertainty
Concerns of Higher Education	Growth and expansion	Accountability, efficiency, and effectiveness	Retrenchment, reduction, and planning
Practice of Institutional Research			
Function	Data collection and analysis	Analysis of evolving management issues	Management, advocacy, and policy research
Structure	Varied, individualized	Second-echelon, consolidated	Consolidated, coordinated, dispersed
Studies	Specific, focused issues: enrollment, space, costs, student characteristics, self-study	Increasingly diverse topics: cost analysis, resource models, evaluation studies	Increasingly broad and diverse topics: planning studies, policy analysis
Methods	Descriptive, quantitative	Specialized techniques, primarily quantitative	Multimethod studies, quantitative and qualitative
Information Systems	Very limited, internal	Management information systems, computerization, data exchange	External, comparative, and microcomputer applications
Profession of Institutional Research			
Nature of the Profession	Discussion forum	Quasi-profession	Reassessment

Table 1. The Evolution of Institutional Research: Practice, Profession, and Association (*continued*)

	1950s and 1960s: Emergence of Institutional Research	*1970s: Growth and Consolidation*	*1980s: Fragmentation and Uncertainty*
Primary Concern	Status and research role; theory and practice; independent management	Integrating new methods and approaches	Dealing with specialized interests and diversity
Member Identification	Invitational	Primary affiliation	Increasingly inclusive
Motivations	Discovering peers and sharing problems	Professional identification, growth and development	Professional advancement, growth and development
Preparation	Varied fields, no formal training	Varied fields, some formal and in-service opportunities	Varied fields, increased in-service training
Association of Institutional Research			
Major Focus	Organizing and attaining stability	Managing growth of the field and the association	Assessing direction, integrating diversity
Major Initiatives	First forums	Expanded forums	Comprehensive forums
	Formalization of the AIR	Formation of the central office	Establishment of the purposes commission
	Newsletter, directory, and special publications	Publications program; state, regional, and special-interest groups; international interest; placement service	Professional development activities; expanded state and regional programs; consultant service

In the late 1950s and early 1960s, the Western Interstate Commission on Higher Education (WICHE), the New England Board of Higher Education (NEBHE), the Southern Regional Education Board (SREB), and the ACE sponsored a variety of workshops on and surveys of institutional research practices and issues. Rourke and Brooks (1966) symbolize the growth of interest in institutional research. These authors describe the growing array of institutional research practices and predict the interest among executive officers in managerial issues that was to emerge in the 1970s. Growth, expansion, and the need for more and better information were driving concerns of our institutions until student discontent at the end of the 1960s disrupted the bigger-is-better bandwagon.

During the late 1950s and 1960s, the practice of institutional research grew with the blessings of many institutional presidents and executive officers. On many campuses, offices of institutional research were established. Often, their staff reported to the president or chief executive officer. Most were small offices whose focus varied with the concerns of the particular institution. The institutional research officers were usually new to the task. They came from various fields (but predominantly the social sciences), they had some prior teaching or administrative experience, and they learned their jobs as they went. While the status of institutional research offices and their place in the institution's organizational structure were varied and changing, the common function was to collect data on important characteristics of the growing institution. Studies tended to be on specific, well-focused issues or concerns—institutional self-study; enrollment and student characteristics; space inventories, needs, and utilization; and budget analysis. The methodology was largely limited to descriptive, quantitative studies using standard data collection procedures and survey techniques. Interest in building a data base was limited to efforts to improve internal record and data collection procedures.

During this period, there seemed to be little concern for the constitution of institutional research as a professional field. The first meetings for institutional researchers were convened by the ACE and by regional consortia to discuss common problems and issues. Even the first AIR forum (1961) was convened by invitation, and many of those who attended saw no need for a permanent organization. Throughout the 1960s, the professional meetings of institutional researchers seemed designed more to promote a discussion forum than to found a tightly integrated field. Discussions among the incumbents of newly created offices centered on ways of solving common problems, on the appropriate organizational status and location of institutional research, and on its appropriate research role: Should it be independent or management-oriented? What was the role of theory in an applied field of practice? Was there a difference between research on a specific institution and on the entire field of higher education? Clearly, the participants' motivations were to discuss these issues and to share their problems and approaches with newly discovered peers at other institutions. Institutional researchers came from diverse fields of preparation, most often the social sciences, and shared neither a common training nor a strong concern about developing such training.

The AIR, as the formal association representing the emerging field of practice, reflected this era. The association became a reality in 1964 when John Stecklein was elected its first president. However, the formation of an association reflected a concern more for creating an organizational mechanism that could conduct the annual meeting, keep track of the growing number of members, and respond to members' interests than for providing professional leadership. For example, the original purposes of the AIR were only to advance research that improves institutions, encourage the application of appropriate methods and techniques, and publish or exchange information about institutions of postsecondary education. They do not reflect a concern for producing publications about institutional research per se or for designing formal professional development activities. Association officers conducted all AIR business from their institutional offices, and the budget was limited (under $30,000 in 1970). However, the growth of the AIR (810 members by 1970), the increase in forum attendance (463 by 1970), and new activities (a newsletter, forum proceedings, annotated bibliographies, and other special publications) began to strain the ability of individual officers to maintain a stable organization, and the merits of establishing a central office began to be discussed. Thus, the first period of institutional research was marked by the rapid emergence of a new institutional role and of a group of practitioners seeking colleagues and direction and by the creation of an organization that could serve their needs but not necessarily establish a professional enterprise.

Growth and Consolidation: The 1970s. Concerns about institutional size and student discontent in the late 1960s and early 1970s reinforced the view that more and better student and educational research, studies of institutional climate, and other forms of institutional self-study were needed. However, the economic recession of the mid 1970s introduced higher education to a new concern—to do more with less. Enrollments would continue to grow, but the rate would slow. Financial resources became increasingly constrained. By the late 1970s, inflation was adding to the financial pressure. Throughout the decade, state agencies of higher education and other external, often government-related groups demanded greater accountability as they became more sophisticated in gathering and analyzing data about higher education and in asking difficult management questions. An era that began with student discontent and prospects for an educational revolution that promised to raise significant educational issues became instead a decade of increasing concern for prudent management and accountability that focused on efficiency and effectiveness in higher education. Are our costs too high? Are we accomplishing our educational goals? Can we account for our resources and performance?

The practice of institutional research mirrored the pressure for prudent financial management and accountability. While some practitioners maintained pretensions of autonomy or independence, institutional researchers on most campuses became primarily management-oriented. Many directors of institutional research came to view themselves as members of the management team. Offices on most campuses were formally established as second- or third-echelon. Increasingly, institutional research was organized as a consolidated office, and relationships to executive officers, staff offices, other campus constituent groups, and even state agencies or external groups were increasingly well defined. On large campuses, institutional research offices added staff and expanded their scope of activities. While continuing the descriptive studies mentioned previously, they began to conduct sophisticated cost and productivity studies, faculty and program evaluations, and studies of student development and to use resource analysis and projection models. Directors also took an active role in the design and development of management information systems, including computerized applications. They often assumed extensive external data-reporting responsibilities, and they participated in data exchange networks related to institutional issues. Despite the increasingly comprehensive array of activities, the increasingly diverse types of studies, and the increasing complexity of the analytic and research methods employed, most institutional research activity continued to be quantitative and management oriented, which led Lyman Glenny in his AIR forum address (1975) to identify institutional researchers with the increasing array of technocrats in higher education.

As a group, institutional researchers were increasingly identified by others as a quasi-professional group recognized for their analytic and research skills. Their own professional concerns seemed to shift from issues of status and research identity to concerns for integrating the many new methods and approaches to the study of management problems. They adopted the AIR as the primary professional association with which to identify, and at meetings they began to seek opportunities for personal development in workshops, seminars, and even state or regional groups. As institutional researchers began to come from increasingly diverse fields (management, information sciences, operations research) many large offices became increasingly concerned about on-the-job training. A few universities also developed programs to train institutional researchers.

At the association level, the AIR spawned a broad array of services that recognized the increasingly professional character and concerns of its members as well as their growing numbers. A national office, with Jean Chulak as the first permanent executive secretary, was established at Florida State University in 1974. The annual forum grew not only in attendance (862 by 1980) but in complexity. Major speakers, contributed papers, panels, and seminars were included to provide diverse program formats in response to the increasing concern among members for professional growth and development opportunities. A publications board instituted in 1974 initiated a differentiated publications program. The *New Directions for Institutional Research* sourcebooks published by Jossey-Bass examined important developments in the field. A cosponsored journal, *Research in Higher Education,* became a vehicle for research articles related to the field, while the *Professional File* series discussed new methods and techniques useful in institutional research. State and regional groups addressing members' needs in geographic areas and special-interest groups designed to bring members with common interests together at forums proliferated. Following the annual forum in Montreal in 1977, the AIR became more seriously international by forming an international affairs committee; it began to foster a small but growing international membership, and it encouraged the development of a very successful European AIR affiliation, which now sponsors its own annual meetings.

Clearly, during the 1970s institutional research witnessed growth and consolidation at all levels. As higher education tried to resolve its NCHEMian dilemma—to manage or not manage?—formally organized offices of institutional research appeared on many campuses. These offices responded to their institution's management problems, an identity with and concern for professional development among AIR members, and an association with a growing set of activities to serve the new quasi-profession.

Fragmentation and Uncertainty: 1980-1985. By the late 1970s, higher education began to address the reality that long-term enrollment declines were imminent, that the financial constraints were not likely to abate, and that emphasis on improved management—improved accountability, efficiency, and effectiveness—was not sufficient for the decade ahead. Institutions began to struggle with retrenchment, reduction, and reallocation. Higher education managers now asked questions not just about efficiency and effectiveness but about priorities and whether the right educational programs for the future were being provided. Others outside the institutions were challenging the quality of our efforts. At the same time, the microcomputer revolution was changing both the administration and educational practices of our institutions. These changes caused some institutional leaders to raise questions about the appropriateness of their current educational direction and about redefinition of that mission.

Once again, the practice of institutional research was not immune to the institutional pressures. While institutional research remained oriented toward management issues, it changed in other ways. Pressures of reduction and reallocation among the institutions within a system or among the units in a large institution often caused several competing units to conduct institutional research studies of their own. Each took an advocacy approach defending its own position rather than striving for detached, objective analysis. Such political uses of institutional research were not new, but they become much more prominent under the conditions just outlined.

Concern for priorities and planning studies increased the emphasis on policy studies emanating from a planning officer. The tendency on some campuses to separate planning and policy analysis from institutional research, the tendency of individual units to do their own research in defence against reductions, and the advent of microcomputers, which allowed units to conduct their own studies and analyses, contributed to the dispersion of institutional research into many offices or administrative units, thereby somewhat reversing the trend of the 1970s toward increasingly centralized or coordinated institutional research activity. The emphasis on planning, reduction, or both required an increased emphasis on institutional and program reviews, planning studies and policy analyses, externally and futures-oriented studies. Such research often requires comprehensive, multimethod studies that use both quantitative and qualitative research measures and techniques. Such research also requires institutional research offices to pay more attention to the use of comparative data (often from other institutions) when determining reduction priorities and to the use of external data on environmental conditions in conducting planning studies. These developments required training institutional researchers in new methodological skills or adding new personnel who possessed such skills.

As a group, institutional researchers seem to be reassessing the nature of their own professional identity. The inclusion of researchers with planning, policy analysis, and evaluation interests; debates about the role of qualitative as well as quantitative techniques; and the emergence of individuals with analytic skills and capability in various offices at both system and institutional levels have fostered discussions about appropriate paths for career advancement, increased the demand for more diverse and specialized personnel, and increased interest in professional development oriented toward planning and the effective use of information technology and microcomputers.

As an association, the AIR has become concerned about how to integrate an increasingly diverse membership. New association activities have been designed to make the forums even more comprehensive (professional development seminars and workshops and tracts for vendors and exhibitors have been added), to expand state and regional programming, and to develop a consulting service. After forum attendance peaked in 1980 and membership began to decline in 1982, the AIR also began to examine its own direction. A special commission was established in 1982 to assess the purposes and direction of the association. In 1984, it made ten recommendations for changes in most aspects of the association, and the executive committee began to discuss a strategy for the future.

These developments of the last five years all suggest that institutional research may fragment on many campuses after a decade of consolidation or improved coordination. Professionals who identify with the field are becoming increasingly diverse in their expertise and interests, and the AIR is becoming increasingly concerned about its own diversity. This fragmentation is combined with some uncertainty about where the field of practice now is and about where it should be headed, about the professional nature of the field and about who the individuals identified with it are and should be, and about the role that the association can or should play.

Challenges for the Future: Transition or Transformation

If one looks at the history sketched briefly in this chapter, one can make several observations: First, the growth of the practice of institutional research, its development as a profession, and the development of the AIR are closely intertwined. Second, both the field and the profession have expanded as members successfully responded to institutional needs for more than two-and-one-half decades. Third, because the AIR is so intertwined with the practice and the profession of institutional research, it has responded effectively to the needs of its members and promoted the growth of a professional identity by emphasizing activities designed to disseminate information about issues and developments in the field and by offering opportunities for professional growth and development to its members. However, its role has been more reactive than proactive. That is, it has tended more to adapt to changes quickly than to set a direction for a rapidly changing field. Fourth, institutional needs and the offices conducting institutional research studies or activities; the types of studies and the methods applied; the backgrounds, needs, and interests of professional members; and association activities and services are all becoming increasingly diverse. They exert strong forces that can fragment the practice, the profession, and potentially even the association.

It is easy to assume that the AIR and its members will once again make the transition by adapting to the current retrenchment and planning demands that are reshaping the field. Such a transitional strategy assumes that the current pattern of fragmentation will not continue and that any changes in the future will not require a radical transformational strategy that places the emphasis on proactive attempts to further the development of the profession and to develop a new way of thinking about the field.

In Chapter Two, Cameron Fincher probes the art and science of this emerging profession and assesses its stage of development. Chapters Three, Four, and Five examine the nature of the environmental forces that are reshaping our institutions and the practice of institutional research. Chapter Six asks whether a reactive transition or a proactive transformation is better suited to making institutional research a viable function for institutional improvement in the years ahead.

References

Brumbaugh, A. J. *Research Designed to Improve Institutions of Higher Learning.* Washington, D.C.: American Council on Education, 1960.

Cowley, W. H. "Two-and-a-Half Centuries of Institutional Research." In R. G. Axt and H. T. Spranger (Eds.), *College Self-Study: Lectures on Institutional Research.* Boulder, Colo.: Western Interstate Commission on Higher Education, 1959.

Doi, J. I. "The Beginnings of a Profession." In R. G. Cope (Ed.), *Professional Development for Institutional Research.* New Directions for Institutional Research, no. 23. San Francisco: Jossey-Bass, 1979.

Glenny, L. "Institutional Research in a Postsecondary World." In R. Cope (Ed.), *Information for Decisions in Postsecondary Education: AIR Forum Proceedings*. Tallahassee, Fla.: Association of Institutional Research, 1975.

Peterson, M. W. "Institutional Research and Policy Formulation: A Contingency Model." In C. Steward (Ed.), *Institutional Research and Policy Formulation: AIR Forum Proceedings*. Tallahassee, Fla.: Association of Institutional Research, 1971.

Peterson, M. W. "IR in Transition, Fragmentation or Integration." In S. Larsen (Ed.), *The Future of Institutional Research*. Raleigh: Southern Association for Institutional Research, North Carolina State University, 1979.

Rourke, F. E., and Brooks, G. E. *The Managerial Revolution in Higher Education*. Baltimore, Md.: Johns Hopkins University Press, 1966.

Marvin W. Peterson is director of the Center for the Study of Higher Education Management at the University of Michigan. He is now president of the Association of Institutional Research.

Institutional research is not a science, and it does not need to be. It is a practicing art with commendable promise as a professional technical speciality in policy-related research.

The Art and Science of Institutional Research

Cameron Fincher

There are two undeniable facts about higher education: Colleges and universities must keep numerous records, and they must report voluminous data to governing, funding, accrediting, and regulating authorities. The analysis and interpretation of institutional records and data, plus the occasional or periodic studies that are necessary to supplement routine record keeping and reporting, would thus seem to be what institutional research is all about.

The origins of institutional research are embedded, therefore, in institutional functions and activities. The organization and governance of English colleges were no doubt an object of study by the colonial colleges established in America, but there was no concept of systematic research to give guidance to such efforts. Tom Dyer (1978) calls historians the first institutional researchers, because they were the first to study charters, presidential correspondence, recorded minutes, and other institutional records for the purpose of depicting the historical development of institutions.

Institutional research as a specialized administrative function begins with the efforts of institutions to use tools and techniques developed in other fields of specialization to study their internal activities and processes. The University of Minnesota, the prime example, established in 1924 a committee on educational research to study the problems of curriculum, student attrition, counseling, and test performance (Gray, 1951). In the following decade, a bureau of institutional research was established for the explicit purpose of conducting studies to facilitate administrative and instructional effectiveness.

Of all the documents pertaining to institutional research, Brumbaugh's (1960) monograph for the American Council on Education (ACE) is the one undeniable classic. A statement issued by the ACE's Office of Statistical Information and Research, headed at that time by Elmer D. West, it specifies the purposes and intents of institutional research. Brumbaugh was appreciative of the forthcoming increase in enrollments that colleges and universities had to prepare for, the rising costs of higher education, the increased complexity of administration, the expansion of institutional programs and services, and the need to convince state legislators that increases in appropriations would be needed.

Administrative effectiveness in dealing with the changing conditions of higher education was, according to Brumbaugh, a matter of asking the right questions and of finding the right answers. Whether the right answers were specific or comprehensive, they depended on the kind of data that only institutional research could provide. Thus, institutional research should play an important role in institutional policy making, planning, management, and evaluation. Institutional research was needed in these areas: goals and objectives, student characteristics and achievement, faculty characteristics and conditions of service, curricular change and effectiveness, institutional administration and organization, funding and financing, and public relations.

A Science of Institutions?

Six years after Brumbaugh's espousal of institutional research, Henry Dyer (1966) asked whether institutional research could ever lead to a science of institutions. Dyer noted the published research dealing with institutional concerns and issues and mentioned the newly formed Association for Institutional Research (AIR) as a professional society. Dyer thought there was cause for optimism if institutional research could reconcile the conflicting points of view represented by Nevitt Sanford (1962) and John Dale Russell. Sanford (1962) was cited as the foremost exponent of long-term, theoretically oriented research into institutional processes and outcomes, while Russell's many writings were typical of studies concerned with practical and purely operational problems. It was Dyer's judgment that institutional research had nowhere to go if it remained purely operational. At the same time, institutional research would be of little help to policy makers and decision makers if it served only to spin theories.

In many respects, the distinction that Dyer was making was a distinction between discipline-oriented and mission-oriented research. However, a bridge could be built between the two by recognizing the centrality of measurement and by developing suitable instruments for the assessment of institutional goals and the degree to which they were being met. Dyer wrote at a time when the Educational Testing Service had launched an ambitious program involving measures of campus climate, faculty and student perceptions of instructional effectiveness, and factors facilitating or impeding institutional progress toward the fulfillment of its goals. His concluding point was that institutional research could lead to a science of institutions if it could deal with "the real problems of particular institutions" and if it endeavored "to fit these problems into some sort of evolving generalizations" (Dyer, 1966, p. 466).

Unfortunately, Dyer did not inquire into the nature of institutions, and he was not explicit about science as either a body of organized facts or an organized search for explanatory concepts and principles. He doubted that institutional research could use experimental methods to good advantage, and he suggested that institutional researchers could serve well by reminding college administrators and faculty of the many blind assumptions on which their work was based. Dyer's contribution is best regarded, therefore, as the challenge he issued and as the support that he gave to the development of assessment instruments and methods.

Changing Problems and Issues. The challenge that Dyer issued was not heard by institutional researchers for many reasons. Neither the 1960s nor the 1970s proved to be years in which a science of educational institutions could be developed. By 1968, other concerns and issues were dominant, and as the 1970s opened, the political, legal, and financial problems of higher education dominated institutional research, just as they dominated other educational functions and activities. Virtually all institutions sought economic, judicial, and technological solutions to their problems, not the self-understanding or self-enlightenment that a science of institutions would presumably bring. The purely operational problems of institutional accountability, management, financing, and evaluation pushed studies of student and faculty characteristics, institutional missions and goals, instructional improvement, and curricular change to the side. Theoretically oriented research became a luxury that few institutions could afford, and administrative officials cited economists, lawyers, and engineers more often than they did the social and behaviorial scientists who had contributed to Sanford's (1962) ambitious volume.

Although the federal government continued to support the development of offices of institutional research in smaller institutions, it shifted its funding policies and priorities to planning, management, and evaluation. Many institutional researchers settled into supportive or technical assistance roles that were necessary for crisis management, the demands of annual budgeting cycles, and the incessant requests for information from governing boards and regulatory agencies. Some directors of institutional research were promoted to vice-presidencies in charge of institutional research and planning, but a large number of institutional researchers became troubleshooters, brushfire fighters, or faceless technocrats. If a few recovered from their newfound obscurity in time to become members of the anonymous leadership described by Lyman Glenny (1972), too many institutional researchers remained the captives of national and statewide demands for data that were uniformly reported for purposes of aggregation. Analytic and interpretative skills did not become tools of the trade for many institutional researchers, and the massive data reported to external authorities did not become a body of knowledge common to all members of a research speciality or profession.

Changing Methods of Inquiry. The early emphasis on student behavior and performance was one of the first casualties for the first generation of institutional researchers. The evaluation of student performance by teaching faculty gave way to the evaluation of teaching effectiveness by student ratings. The personal, social, and academic characteristics of students became objects of large-scale research efforts by national agencies and associations, and predictive studies of academic performance became a service rendered routinely by national testing agencies. If their institutions participated, institutional researchers could obtain far more data on students from the American Council on Education's Cooperative Institutional Research Program than they could by their own methods. And, as more institutions adopted open-door or nonselective admissions policies, the determinants of academic performance became less an object of research at the institutional level.

Faculty work load studies continued to show occasional interest in instructional methods and outcomes but more or less stablized as analyses of faculty activities. Assigned time for instruction, research, and public service became a standardized form of reporting to centralized governing or coordinating bodies, and faculty contact hours, student credit hours, or both became the sole measure of faculty productivity at too many institutions. Analyses of financial budgetary data, space utilization, and enrollment projections became the dominant if not exclusive concern of many offices of institutional research. And, a generation of institutional researchers became quite productive in the 1970s without ever having read or even heard of Sanford's (1962) psychological and social interpretation of higher learning in American.

Seen in this light, the development of institutional research in the years following its early, enthusiastic beginnings was greatly influenced by events and forces outside offices of institutional research. The centralization of administrative and governing authority within the separate states, the presence of the federal government as a funding and regulatory agency, and the extensive analysis of higher education by national commissions were potent forces influencing the data-collecting and reporting activities of institutional researchers. Also relevant to objective and systematic research at the institutional level was the changing climate in which institutional studies had to be conducted. Student protests and faculty dissent placed many barriers between researchers and those who were no longer willing to be objects of research. Court rulings and fears of litigation declared many interesting research questions out of bounds.

Models of Varying Influence

The advocacy of other models and paradigms was particularly strong in the late 1960s and early 1970s. Unifying or organizing themes for institutional research as a developing professional specialty were not highly visible, and institutional research was regarded by some observers as floundering in its efforts to become a specialized function in academic administration and governance. Institutional researchers were greatly diversified in background and experience, and the success with which they applied various tools of their trade to institutional problems varied even more. Depending on their professional education and training, institutional researchers were inclined to define institutional problems in familiar terms and thereby to advocate the application of methods and techniques that made personal sense. The proceedings of the AIR annual forums thus reflect a variety of insights and viewpoints concerning the future development of institutional research. Insofar as the professional development of institutional research can be traced, institutional researchers seem to have been reluctant to chart courses that would carry them too far from their original moorings.

Educational Research. The oldest role model for institutional researchers was the traditional model of educational research. Despite many efforts to introduce concepts and principles of experimental inquiry into institutional studies, institutional researchers did not identify strongly with educational researchers, and many of them gave up their membership in the American Educational Research Association as they became increasingly active in the Association for Institutional Research. Educational researchers continued to be enamored of basic or fundamental processes in education that were best investigated with experimental or quasi-experimental methods of inquiry and analysis. In contrast, institutional researchers have seen their responsibilities as related to practical, applied, mission-oriented forms of research, and they have been particularly aware of profound differences between the problems of elementary education, where the interests of educational researchers are concentrated, and the problems of higher education. To no small extent, educational research has remained a captive of the natural sciences, although it has yet to produce a science of education. Efforts during the 1960s to redirect educational research to applied, mission-oriented, policy-related forms of research were not successful, despite lavish financial support for regional laboratories, research and development centers, and other extradepartmental research agencies.

From later perspectives, it would appear that institutional researchers were wise not to tie their destiny to that of educational researchers. Neither regional laboratories nor research and development centers could free educational research from orthodoxy, and educational research lost much of its credibility as a means of influencing educational policy. Further retrospection suggests that different funding policies and priorities for educational and institutional research on the part of the federal government virtually assured that the two would not develop along parallel paths (Cronbach and Suppes, 1969; Fincher, 1974; Gideonse, 1968).

Measurement and Assessment. As Dyer (1966) suggested, measurement did not prove to be central for institutional research. Although commendable progress has been made in the development of instruments for the assessment of institutional characteristics, the usefulness of those instruments in the improvement of institutions still remains to be proved. Each college and university has a personality and character of its own, but the extent to which personality and character are accurately depicted in measures of campus climates or environments is unknown. Many crucial features of colleges and universities remain obscure or otherwise concealed from the perceptions of trustees, administrators, faculty, and students as they respond to such instruments as the College and University Environment Scales (CUES), the Institutional Goals Inventory (IGI), and the Institutional Functioning Inventory (IFI). The uses of such instruments depend on the differential weighting that is necessary when the averages of different groups are computed and studied. The significance or importance to be attached to the various dimensions of institutional life raises further questions. And, there are numerous reservations concerning the relevance of national or regional norms for the institution being studied.

Nonetheless, the premises on which the CUES, IGI, and IFI measures were based are sound. Such inventories reflect perceptions, judgments, opinions, or beliefs that are more systematic and objective than the journalistic or impressionistic reports so often publicized in the news media. There are also reasons to believe that, if valid, reliable measures of institutional characteristics can be developed, the possibility of matching institutions and individuals for their mutual benefit improves. If such measures are used wisely in advising and counseling students, they should facilitate the educational accomplishment of those students. Unfortunately, the institutional characteristics tapped by such instruments may be more subtle and thereby less accessible to systematic inquiry than the developers expected.

Systems Analysis. The influence of systems analysis on the development of institutional research is appreciable, but a high level of sophistication in systems thinking is not obvious in many institutional researchers. Systems concepts and principles were evident in the centralization of administration and governance during the 1960s and in the need for geographical distribution of educational resources and opportunities. Systems analysis also laid the groundwork for the computer and communications revolution that swept college campuses at the same time. Cutbacks in the nation's space program presumably brought more systems analysts to college campuses and thereby fostered further adaptation of systems thinking for institutions of higher education (Hoos, 1972).

For institutions of higher education, the introduction of systems theory and concepts may be the best example of efforts to transfer technology from one organizational setting to another. In whatever way systems design and engineering may have been serviceable for corporate industry and for the nation's space program, much of their effectiveness was lost on institutions that had other kinds of traditions and commitments. Sufficient attention was not always paid to the differences between corporate industry or business and educational institutions, and efforts to transfer specific concepts and techniques without modification or adaptation resulted in noticeable contradictions. For example, traditions of autonomy and independence prevented units of statewide systems of higher education from functioning as systems theory suggested. Many institutions were members of a statewide or multicampus system for reasons of funding and public support, not because each was an interrelated part of a closed system. Systems thinking may have been more beneficial in defining and discussing the common problems of colleges than in finding solutions to those problems.

Operations Research. Closely related to systems analysis—and rejected for many of the same reasons—are the specialties of operations research and management science. Institutional management and governance have been the subject of occasional research by operations researchers and management scientists, but there is little evidence of an enduring impact on institutional operations and practices. Institutional researchers may remain impervious to influence because they seldom read the professional literature of operations research and management science, and they rarely belong to professional associations representing such research interests. Another reason may be that both operations research and management science are too specialized to serve the practical needs of institutional researchers. Particular tools and techniques may be borrowed when appropriate, and a few concepts would seem to be common to the three fields, but for the most part institutional researchers have not identified their own interests with those of operational researchers or management scientists. Neither the research skills nor the research interests of institutional researchers would appear to be as tightly knit as those of operational researchers and management scientists. However, operations research and management science do involve resources, methods, and facilities that institutional researchers believe to be missing from their own field (Schroeder and Adams, 1976).

Evaluation Research. The influence of evaluation research as a role model is difficult to assess. The evaluation of educational programs and services is not incompatible with institutional research, but evaluation research on college and university campuses has not originated in offices of institutional research. The concern for evaluation research dates from the specific requirements for program evaluation contained in federal legislation of the 1960s. Many aspects of evaluation have always been indigenous to education and a visible component of educational research, with the result that institutional research has sometimes been perceived by faculty as evaluation in another guise. Nonetheless, the relevance of evaluation research for institutional researchers may be found in its differences from traditional modes of educational research and in its immediate applications to many problems and issues in institutional research. By 1980, there was no doubt that evaluation research had emerged as a research specialty in its own right, while institutional research was still uncertain about many of its merits. The need for program and project evaluation in higher education was quite evident when higher education was in its period of rapid growth, but that need was not recognized fully until institutions were confronting uncertain enrollments and possibilities of retrenchment. A continuing demand for evaluation thus may mean that institutional researchers will become increasingly involved in program evaluation and assessment regardless of how much they prefer other duties and responsibilities (Fincher, 1981).

Computer Modeling. Although computer modeling is closely related to operations research and management science, it has had a different kind of relationship with institutional research. During the late 1960s, the promise for computer-based models of colleges and universities was quite high, and as early as 1965, CAMPUS (Comprehensive Analytical Methods for Planning in University/College Systems) was discussed in institutional research circles. By the early 1970s, HELP/PLANTRAN (Higher Education Long-Range Planning/Planning Translator), SEARCH (System for Evaluating Alternative Resource Commitments in Higher Education), and RRPM (Resource Requirements Prediction Model) were on the scene. Computer models had three advantages: They made it possible to forecast or project future conditions in institutional development, they allowed researchers to ask questions about contingent events or situations, and they promoted the understanding of the many complex variables that were involved in institutional management. By simulating institutional activities and functions, computer models foreshadowed a science of institutional management that would enable institutional leaders to study the cause-and-effect relations of their administrative decisions and policies. With the development of realistic simulation models, administrators could anticipate changes in financing, student enrollments, faculty supply and demand, curicular needs, and public expectations. A means of monitoring and managing complex and interrelated institutional functions was almost at hand (Mason, 1976).

Computer modeling failed to live up to its promise for many reasons (Greenberger and others, 1976). The difficulties of updating models and keeping them current were sufficient to explain most failures, but even more obvious explanations are found in the changing environment of higher education and in the lack of receptivity shown by institutional leaders. The financial crisis of the early 1970s called attention to the high cost of simulation and modeling, and the downturn in student enrollments was a disrupting variable that enrollment-driven models could not easily accommodate. The data banks of such models reflected institutional growth and expansion, not conditions of decline or steady state. Many academic administrators remained optimistic about the uses of computer models but did not report extensive use of computer-based information in the administrative decisions of their own institutions (Plourde, 1976). However, the advent of microcomputers in recent years has revitalized computer applications on college campuses, and the promise for decision support systems reached an all-time high in the 1980s.

Planning Models. Although institutional researchers have never identified themselves explicitly as planners, they have been influenced by planning principles and practices. As campus planning agencies fulfilled their mission in the 1970s, mergers with offices of institutional research were not unknown. Despite their many affinities, the AIR and the Society for College and University Planning (SCUP) did not seriously consider merger, but the continued separateness was a function of leadership, not of incompatible purposes and programs. Both the AIR and the SCUP owe much to the statewide master planning that was prominent in the 1960s, and they both reflect a renewed interest in program planning and development as conditions in higher education signal a return to systemwide and even statewide needs and considerations.

Program Budgeting. Also evident in the early 1980s was a continuing need for financial and budgetary analyses that supported institutional and program planning. For many years, institutional research documented the declining support for higher education from the federal government, the low probability that institutions of higher education would obtain an increased proportion of state and local resources, and the widespread need for colleges and universities to seek other sources of funding for continued institutional development. The formula budgeting that had prevailed in the 1960s was no longer the fortunate means of financing public higher education, and different funding methods were needed to cope with the conditions that adversely affected institutions in financial or budgetary difficulty. The analysis of institutional income and expenditures, one of the first responsibilities of offices of institutional research, again became a challenge. Uncertain student enrollments, the rising cost of education, government regulations, competition among institutions and agencies, and threats of a taxpayer revolt were the obvious features of that challenge (Gross, 1983; Mingle and others, 1981).

Measured Outcomes. As institutional researchers became increasingly involved in financial and budgetary analysis, they became increasingly concerned about measured outcomes that could be related to educational costs. The public demand for good measures of educational outcomes can be dated from the Equal Educational Opportunity Study (Coleman and others, 1966) and the various reanalyses of the data collected in that study (Jencks and others, 1972; Mayeske and others, 1972). The financial crisis of the early 1970s added impetus to the accountability movement and placed institutional researchers under considerable pressure to adopt the tools and techniques of econometrics. There was a strenuous challenge to measure in economic terms the outcomes of higher education and to demonstrate their cost-effectiveness in ways that would satisfy national leaders and critics. Among the techniques recommended for this responsibility were input-output analysis, linear programming, game theory, and econometric modeling.

Efforts to study the productivity of colleges and universities with economic methods were less than satisfactory for both institutional researchers and institutional leaders. The cost-effectiveness of a college education was not easy to compute, because neither costs nor indicators of effectiveness could be systematically and consistently derived. Institutions of higher education were not industrial plants, and the productive function studied by economists in other organizational settings did not make sense for colleges and universities. Bowen (1977) effectively answered econometric critics by demonstrating the importance of nonmonetary outcomes in the form of numerous benefits and advantages to both society and individual college graduates. However, the analysis of educational outcomes in terms of input and process variables remained a challenge that institutional researchers should learn to understand. Cost-benefit analysis is still a worthy application of the institutional researcher's time, and the demonstration of educational benefits and advantages is still the most effective argument that can be made to the critics of education.

Policy Research and Anaysis. Throughout the 1970s, there was growing awareness that the functions and activities of institutional research were determined for the most part by public policy at national, regional, and state levels. Federal policies and funding changed drastically as national administrations changed and as national priorities shifted to economic, energy, and environmental issues. State policies and priorities underwent similar changes as state governments and coordinating boards assumed additional financial burdens for education, coped with stagflation, and addressed their own energy and environmental issues. Institutional policies changed as national and state policies required attention to diminishing public resources and to reallocation of resources among competing sectors of the economy and competing institutions of higher education.

Unfortunately, institutional researchers were seen in too many institutions as data collectors who could contribute neither substance nor style to institutional policy making. They were, in Wilensky's (1969) terminology, facts-and-figures people, not internal communications specialists or contact people. By this time, many directors of institutional research were removed from the top level of administration and reported to vice-presidents who were not always involved in the formation of crucial institutional policy. Whenever institutional researchers were participants in institutional policy making or influential with administrators who were, their participation and influence could often be attributed to personal working relations that had been established in the past.

Nonetheless, policy research and analysis gave institutional research a focus that Brumbaugh (1960) and others had specified. Policy-related research in particular offered a context in which institutional researchers could assert their professional status and in which their specialized skills and competencies could come into play. There were excellent reasons to believe that the meaning and significance of institutional research could be found in the systematic, empirical technical assistance that institutional researchers could provide in the formation of viable institutional policy. It was again possible to think of institutional researchers as problem solvers who, by virtue of the data and information at their disposal, could contribute to policy and decision making as deliberative processes. As Table 1 shows, the methodological influences on institutional research have varied appreciably with time and circumstances.

Institutional Research as Science

If institutional research is correctly identified as a specialized administrative function that dates from 1960, give or take three or four years, what can be said about its specialized, advanced, or professional status a quarter of a century later? Institutional researchers would be reluctant to claim prominent status among traditional fields of disciplined inquiry, but they could point to an appreciable array of methods, skills, and competencies that are applied in pursuit of interesting knowledge. They could contend seriously that institutional

Table 1. Methodological Influences in Institutional Research

The Early Years: 1958–1967	The Crisis Years: 1968–1973	The Later Years: 1974–1985
Long-range planning	Planning, programming, budgeting systems	Strategic planning
Student characteristics		Student program needs
Faculty activities	Evaluation research	Mission review, marketing, recruitment
Enrollment studies	Faculty evaluation	
Admission and placement studies	Demographic forecasting	Measured outcomes
	Economic benefits	Utilization of capital facilities
Space utilization studies	Cost studies	Needs assessment
Institutional studies	Management information systems	Effective information systems
Self-studies for accreditation	Management by objectives	Program assessment
Income/expenditures analysis	Zero-based budgeting	Reduction-in-force
	Resource allocation and utilization	Policy analysis
		Budgeting strategies and priorities
		Decision support systems
		Administrative staff needs

research has not aspired to be a science as physics, chemistry, and biology are. On the contrary, institutional research has not been influenced by the natural sciences as much as it has applied the concepts and methods of other sciences to various institutional problems. Thus, few institutional researchers would claim that Henry Dyer's (1966) goal of a science of institutions has been achieved, and most would be skeptical that such as aspiration is a worthy one.

There are reasons, nonetheless, to examine the scientific underpinnings of institutional research. Other fields of specialization are judged by the sophistication of their theoretical bases, methods of investigation, and the empirical findings that systematic inquiry has netted; institutional research need not be an exception. There was a need for theoretically based studies in 1983, as there was in 1963. There is also a need for sophisticated methods of inquiry and analysis that can derive right answers for the right questions, as Brumbaugh (1960) indicated twenty-five years ago. And, there are many reasons for assessing the current state of knowledge in institutional research as the outcome of twenty-five years of investigation into the internal operations and processes of higher education.

Theoretical Bases. The conceptual, ideational bases of institutional research would be judged by most knowledgeable critics as lacking strength and internal consistency. The efforts of institutional research to solve institutional problems and to study internal processes are not guided by a conspicuous network of hypotheses and conjectures that could be called theory. Colleges and universities are remarkably diverse institutions, and despite many similarities in structure and functions, there are few useful generalizations that would apply to all. Although occasional attempts are made at theory building in higher education, most institutions have a justifiable claim to the uniqueness that they profess in the presence of evaluation committees, prospective students, and newspaper reporters. Given the premise that institutional research should be the systematic, objective study of internal operations and processes, it follows that neither institutional research nor its object of study is best described by its nomothetic or lawlike characteristics. The idiosyncractic features of institutional research dominate, and institutional researchers are better prepared to analyze and interpret specific events and processes within their institutions than they are to explain complex institutional behavior in theoretical terms.

Methods of Inquiry. The strength of institutional research must be found in the methods that institutional researchers have adopted or devised for the analysis and interpretation of institutional data. As institutional records have become increasingly computerized, institutional researchers have gained commendable proficiency as information specialists. Various methods have been developed for the routine reporting functions of colleges and universities, and the aggregation of institutional data for uniform reporting to external authorities is now taken for granted. Methods of statistical, demographic, financial, and budgetary analysis have been applied to the numerous problems of institutional life with valuable results for institutional planning, management, and evaluation. Many institutional researchers are able to deal with the diversities of administrative, business and financial, faculty, and student records, and some have a remarkable expertise in relating computer applications to the problems and issues of higher education.

The extent to which institutional researchers have developed their own methods and techniques is an open question. Other fields have developed the statistical and quasi-experimental methods that institutional researchers use. Their methods of financial and budgetary analysis were developed elsewhere, and their measures of student characteristics, performance, and academic progress have been developed mostly by national testing or research agencies. However, the products of the National Center for Higher Education Management Systems (NCHEMS) have been influenced by institutional researchers (Lawrence and Service, 1977), and some institutional researchers have been particularly resourceful in the analysis of faculty work loads and productivity, in studies of student development, and in the development of planning methods and models. Given the reactive stance that colleges and universities assumed during the years in which institutional research developed, it is easy to infer that institutional researchers have not been encouraged to design and improve their own methods of inquiry and analysis into institutional problems.

Empirical Findings. Institutional research has produced volumes of institutional studies, research reports, journal articles, conference proceedings, workshop manuals, hardback books, and handbooks, but only reservations can be expressed concerning the establishment of an organized body of knowledge common to all practitioners in the field. Several sources of knowledge based on institutional research are national in scope and provide both cross sectional and longitudinal data for institutional analysis. The Cooperative Institutional Research Program (CIRP) launched by the American Council of Education in 1964, the Higher Education General Information Survey (HEGIS) conducted by the federal government, and other national surveys, such as the digests and projections of educational statistics produced by the National Center for Education Statistics, provide valuable backgrounds against which institutional trends and developments can be viewed. The AIR forum proceedings, its *Professional File* series, the journal *Research in Higher Education,* and the Jossey-Bass *New Directions in Institutional Research* sourcebooks give institutional researchers an opportunity to publish research results and findings of common interest. An annual forum for European AIR members provides further opportunities for the discussion of common interests and reflects the diversity of research findings.

However, despite the mass of data and information now available, institutional research is still not characterized by empirical findings that resemble the uniformities and regularities found in other areas of specialization. Institutional researchers share many common research skills and interests, but there is no core of hard-and-fast, systemic truths that each must master in becoming an institutional researcher. Newcomers to the field are still drawn from various academic and professional backgrounds, and, despite appreciable efforts by the AIR to provide training and developmental opportunities through workshops and forums, institutional researchers remain a highly diverse collegial group (Schietinger, 1968; Dressel and Associates, 1971; Dressel and Pratt, 1971; Jedamus and others, 1980).

Institutional Research as Art

If institutional research has been slow to develop as a specialty with scientific underpinnings, what can be said about its growth as a professional or technical specialty that might qualify as a performing art? Since *art* means "a specific skill or its application" and "any craft, trade, or profession" as well as the "making or doing of things that display form, beauty, and unusual perception" (*Webster's New World Dictionary*, 1980), the question is not out of order.

As an art, craft, or profession, there is much about institutional research that is not in doubt. Most institutional research studies are applied, mission-oriented investigations of practical institutional problems. As a rule, they address specific concerns or issues within the institution, and they are said to be conducted on an ad hoc basis. Thus, the results or outcomes of institutional research are usually specific to the institution, and they may not be generalizable to other institutions of similar size or structure. As institutional researchers quickly learn, the findings and conclusions of institutional studies at one institution may not be transferable to other institutions even within the same statewide system.

The professional and technical status of institutional research as an art can be examined in several ways. The methodological sophistication of institutional researchers can be examined in this light, and other characteristics of professional status, such as standards, norms, and institutional impact, should throw additional light on the subject. The conclusions and implications reached in addressing such questions are more or less a definition of the role and functions of institutional research in the 1980s.

Methodological Sophistication. As one form of policy-related research, institutional research in the 1980s is greatly different from the institutional studies conducted in the 1960s. An impressive array of tools and techniques is now available to institutional researchers, and greatly enhanced capabilities in computation and communications permit studies of a scope and depth that were not possible two decades ago. Conceptual distinctions between theory and policy give a better grasp of the methodological differences between theory-based and policy-related research. Theory is now accurately perceived as a conceptual framework of hypotheses and empirical findings that can help to explain observed events and processes. Physical, biological, behavioral, and social sciences traditionally seek to explain significant events or outcomes in terms of their antecedents, and the construction or development of theory is often identified as an attempt to answer the question, How? The preferred outcome of theory is usually a conclusion that extends or elaborates what is known about the objects, conditions, and results being investigated.

In contrast, policy is best perceived as a logical, coherent rationale providing guidance for administrative decisions and actions. The outcome of policy-related research is likely to be an interpretation of observed events, followed by recommendations for improvements, redirection, or other modifications. Frequently, alternatives for action are delineated or fashioned, and the suitability of those alternatives is then judged in terms of their consequences. In this way, there is an active concern for decisions or choices, and policy-related research often seeks an answer to the question, Which? Plans, programs, and deliberate action are typical outcomes of policy-related research in higher education.

Multiple regression techniques give institutional researchers a powerful tool for the analysis of policy variables when policy-related research is clearly their intent. Computer capabilities in most offices of institutional research permit analysis-of-effects designs that relate dependent research variables to the multiple independent variables that are often operative in institutional problems. Whenever the researcher's intent is theory-based research, multiple regression techniques provide partitioning-of-variance designs that are equally helpful in specifying the variance in research outcomes that can be attributed to the researcher's independent or experimental variables. The choice of research models is crucial, therefore, and institutional researchers must take as much care in the definition and measurement of their policy variables as they take in the analysis of their data.

The possibilities for policy-related research are particularly promising to institutional researchers because institutions of higher education are so complex. However, *policy-related research,* not *policy research* or *analysis,* is the correct term, because of the manner in which policy is formulated in educational institutions. Policy is seldom determined by research findings alone, and it is not merely a matter of politics, despite appearances. Whatever the policy-making process is in higher education, it is a deliberative process that pays considerable attention to factual, empirical information. In the absence of such information, most policy makers will fall back on preferences and suppositions. No small challenge to institutional researchers, therefore, is policy-related research that will keep policy makers honest.

In addition to policy-related research, institutional researchers are showing increasing sophistication about funding, financing, and budgeting. The competition of institutions for outside funding adds impetus to the organizational intelligence role of some offices of institutional research. Institutional image is not unrelated to success in fund raising, and institutional research is not irrelevant to the image building of colleges and universities. More important, however, is the sophistication that comes from historical, developmental, and comparative perspectives in higher education. There is appreciable awareness that institutions of higher education must be understood and interpreted in terms of their historical development as well as of their structural and functional features. Institutional reputations are seldom changed dramatically by reorganization, new presidents, curricular revisions, or faculty and student recruitment. On the contrary, reputations can lag behind institutional performance or live on long after performance has declined. Institutional reputations are the results of historical developments, just as institutional research and other institutional functions are.

Standards and Norms. The standards and norms that would accurately reflect the status of institutional research as a profession are still in the process of becoming. The Association for Institutional Research serves many purposes of a professional society, but it has not established standards of training and preparation that can be enforced. Entry into the field of institutional research is still a matter of appointment by presidents or vice-presidents who designate newcomers institutional researchers. Membership in the AIR is still a matter of professional or personal preference, not of professional performance. Although the AIR has made commendable efforts to introduce new members to institutional research concepts and methods, no performance standards have been set for the application and use of those concepts and methods.

Professional norms in institutional research are almost as difficult to establish as professional standards. Several surveys have dealt with the demographics of institutional researchers, and one or two have tapped the functions or activities that constitute their duties and responsibilities. However, the norms of institutional research are difficult to delineate, because they are still in their formative stages. The ambiguity of professional norms strikes many institutional researchers as both typical and healthy.

Institutional Impact. The influence that institutional research has had on the nation's institutions of higher education is, of course, a matter of judgment. Institutional researchers have seen their professional and personal influence ebb and flow with changes in the president's or chancellor's office. Some have witnessed immediate and direct consequences of their influence, while others have served long and diligently without seeing noticeable results of any kind. Yet, it is altogether possible that the most significant and enduring impact of institutional research on institutional operations and practices has been in areas little affected by changes in presidents. This is to say that the impact of institutional research may be more noticeable in institutional operations than in institutional policy.

There are numerous early changes in institutional operations that can be attributed to institutional research and to the presence on campuses of individuals directly concerned with the institution's internal processes. At least one generation of institutional researchers had appreciable influence through their enrollment projections. Others can claim improved efficiency in course sectioning and scheduling, reduction of overlap in course content and requirements, and elimination of small, costly courses. Some can point to improved admission standards and procedures, changes in retention policies and practices, and improvements in use of part-time faculty. Without doubt, institutional research has influenced faculty assignments, the uses of instructional space and facilities, and the specification of faculty and staff workloads.

Later changes that can be attributed to institutional research pertain to institutional planning, management, and evaluation. In planning, institutional research had a noticeable impact on the kinds of data or information gathered for planning purposes and on the manner in which the data were collected. Many of these changes were subtle, and some may have been unavoidable, but systematic planning efforts have always involved the gathering of data, and those who gather data are participants in the planning process. Influence has also been seen in the uses made of data by planning committees or commissions. The interpretation of data often suggests the uses to which they will be put, and planning committees are notoriously weak in analytic and interpretative skills.

There are many ways in which institutional research may have influenced administrative or managerial decisions during the 1960s and 1970s. Much of this influence may have more to do with style than with substance, but the influence has nonetheless been effective. Administrators who were infatuated with management information systems needed help in deciding the kinds of data that should be stored for later retrieval and use. And, as in the case of planning committees, administrators often needed assistance in the interpretation of management information stored and retrieved at their own request. However, the most substantive impact of institutional research is likely to have been on the ways in which administrative decisions were ostensibly made. Some institutional research confirmed more administrative decisions than it informed, but increasingly few administrative decisions were made without some semblance of fact finding.

The influence of institutional research on evaluation is more difficult to trace, but it can be seen in its effect on program review or assessment procedures. The review, assessment, and evaluation of academic programs and funded projects inevitably require some kind of descriptive data that are historical in nature. Institutional researchers often provide this kind of information when registrars, directors of admissions, deans, and department heads cannot. The storage and retrieval of historical data that can serve descriptive, comparative purposes exert a subtle but nonetheless relevant influence on program review or assessment.

Potential if not actual impact is very much the case in the provision of student and academic services, such as academic advisement, student counseling, and career placement. As student demands for these services increase at many colleges, the need for systematic, ongoing review will be intensified. universities in particular may be under pressure to evaluate student services as the cost and the demand for them increase. Academic support services, as components of faculty development programs and as new commitments at many institutions, will also be reviewed or monitored as their costs become visible in institutional budgets and financial reports.

In brief, the institutional impact of institutional research over a twenty-five-year period is pervasive if not prominent. The influence of institutional research is more visible in operational or procedural matters than in administrative decision making and institutional policy, but influence in the last two areas is nonetheless present. Institutional research is undoubtedly one of several forces that have encouraged and facilitated participatory decision making in administrative councils and open policy deliberations in academic governance.

The Potential for Continued Development

A careful review of the development on institutional research since 1960 undoubtedly discloses its hesitant but commendable progress as a specialized administrative function. Table 2 summarizes the features that suggest the emerging status of institutional research as a practicing profession, and the continuing challenges to the institutions of higher education imply that it may indeed be an indispensable support service for administrative decision making and institutional policy formation. In the 1980s, institutional research is best described as a professional, technical specialty with strong resources and capabilities for policy-related research in institutions of higher education. There is no less need for policy-related research in the 1980s than there was in the 1960s. On the contrary, the need for such research has increased, and institutional researchers should never hesitate to quote or cite Brumbaugh's (1960, p. 34) admonishment: "To make wise decisions, data that only institutional research can provide are indispensable."

However, if institutional research is to realize its potential for continuing professional development, there are numerous challenges that must be met. Institutional research perspectives must be broadened, and they must include more in-depth analyses of colleges and universities as educational institutions and national resources. The historical, developmental, and comparative dimensions of higher education must be better appreciated, and there must be less infatuation with business corporations, government agencies, and other organizations that cannot provide a viable model for colleges to emulate. Henry Dyer's (1966) challenge should again be considered, and the contributions of institutional research to the systematic, coherent study of collegiate institutions should be greatly strengthened.

Institutional research could make an essential contribution by helping to create a climate wherein the study of colleges and universities as societal and cultural institutions would be worthy of its own theoretical bases, methods of inquiry, and empirical findings. Such a contribution should not be made at the expense of the policy-related research that institutional researchers must provide, but a more positive attitude toward theory-related research would accomplish much in the continued development of institutional research.

Table 2. The Developmental Status of Institutional Research

As a Science	
Theoretical Bases	Increasing awareness that institutional research needs a unifying or integrative nexus of ideas that would provide a good theoretical foundation; an absence of well-formulated hypotheses or theorems to be tested experimentally or quasi-experimentally
Methods of Inquiry	Many applications and uses of statistical methods and quasi-experimental design for institutional and program analysis, but an increasing need for methods of inquiry, analysis, and verification that serve institutions of higher education well
Empirical Findings	Massive data and detailed information about institutional activities and functions, but no body of knowledge commonly accepted by institutional researchers as essential to mastery of the field, and limited knowledge of institutional outcomes, productivity, and effectiveness
As an Art	
Methodological Sophistication	Increasing appreciation of both theory and policy, their distinctions, and their relevance for institutional research; methods and techniques that can greatly enhance institutional researchers' analytic and interpretative capabilities
Standards and Norms	Still in the process of becoming, but nonetheless important; a continuing need for AIR leadership in setting standards of preparation, training, and entry to the professional field and in providing newcomers with inservice developmental opportunities
Institutional Impact	Appreciable influence on institutional record keeping and data reporting, with significant impact on style of administrative decision making in large institutions and in centralized boards of governance or coordination; slight influence on faculty governance and participation in institutional management; increasing influence on program planning, review, and evaluation

In conclusion, the merits of institutional research depend not on its scientific underpinnings but on its relevance and influence in decision and policy making. In its young adult years, institutional research makes a substantive contribution to institutional planning management, and there are many conspicuous indications that it is capable of contributing even more.

References

Bowen, H. R. *Investment in Learning: The Individual and Social Value of American Higher Education.* San Francisco: Jossey-Bass, 1977.

Brumbaugh, A. J. *Research Designed to Improve Institutions of Higher Learning.* Washington, D.C.: American Council on Education, 1960.

Coleman, J. S., and others. *Equality of Educational Opportunity.* Washington, D.C.: U. S. Government Printing Office, 1966.

Cronbach, L. J., and Suppes, P. (Eds.). *Research for Tomorrow's Schools: Disciplined Inquiry for Education.* New York: Macmillan, 1969.

Dressel, P. L. "The Shaping of Institutional Research and Planning." *Research in Higher Education,* 1981, *14,* 229-258.

Dressel, P. L., and Associates. *Institutional Research in the University: A Handbook.* San Francisco: Jossey-Bass, 1971.

Dyer, H. S. "Can Institutional Research Lead to a Science of Institutions?" *Educational Record,* 1966, *47,* 452-466.

Dyer, T. G. "Institutional Research and Institutional History." *Research in Higher Education,* 1978, *8,* 283-286.

Fincher, C. "COBRE and the Dilemma of Basic Research in Education." *Educational Researcher,* 1974, *3* (2), 11-13.

Fincher, C. "The Literature of Evaluation Research." *Research in Higher Education,* 1981, *14,* 277-280.

Fincher, C. "The Return of Grand Strategy." *Research in Higher Education,* 1983, *19,* 125-126.

Gideonse, H. D. "Research, Development, and the Improvement of Education." *Science,* 1968, *162,* 541-545.

Glenny, L. A. "The Anonymous Leaders of Higher Education." *Journal of Higher Education,* 1972, *43,* 9-22.

Gray, J. *The University of Minnesota: 1851-1951.* Minneapolis: University of Minnesota Press, 1951.

Greenberger, M., Crenson, M. A., and Crissey, B. L. *Models in the Policy Process: Public Decision Making in the Computer Era.* New York: Russell Sage Foundation, 1976.

Gross, F. M. "Formula Budgeting and the Financing of Public Higher Education: Panacea or Nemesis for the 1980s?" In *Institutional Research Issues and Applications 1978-1983.* AIR Professional File 1-16. Tallahassee, Fla.: Association for Institutional Research, 1983.

Hoos, I. R. *Systems Analysis in Public Policy: A Critique.* Berkeley: University of California Press, 1972.

Jedamus, P., Peterson, M. W., and Associates. *Improving Academic Management: A Handbook of Planning and Institutional Research.* San Francisco: Jossey-Bass, 1980.

Jencks, C., and others. *Inequality: A Reassessment of the Effect of Family in America.* New York: Basic Books, 1972.

Lawrence, G. B., and Service, A. L. (Eds.). *Quantitative Approaches to Higher Education Management.* ERIC/Higher Education Research Report No. 4. Washington, D.C.: American Association for Higher Education, 1977.

Mason, T. R. (Ed.). *Assessing Computer-Based System Models.* New Directions for Institutional Research, no. 9. San Francisco: Jossey-Bass, 1976.

Mayeske, G. A., and others. *A Study of Our Nation's Schools.* Washington, D.C.: U. S. Government Printing Office, 1972.

Mingle, J. R., and Associates. *Challenges of Retrenchment: Strategies for Consolidating Programs, Cutting Costs, and Reallocating Resources.* San Francisco: Jossey-Bass, 1981.

Plourde, P. J. "Institutional Use of Models: Hope or Continued Frustration?" In T. R. Mason (Ed.), *Assessing Computer-Based System Models.* New Directions for Institutional Research, no. 9. San Francisco: Jossey-Bass, 1976.

Sanford, N. (Ed.). *The American College: A Psychological and Social Interpretation of the Higher Learning.* New York: Wiley, 1962.

Schietinger, E. F. (Ed.). *Introductory Papers on Institutional Research.* Atlanta: Southern Regional Education Board, 1968.

Schroeder, T. G., and Adams, C. R. "The Effective Use of Management Science in University Administration." *Review of Educational Research,* 1976, *46,* 117-131.

Webster's New World Dictionary of the American Language: Second College Edition. New York: Simon & Schuster, 1980.

Wilensky, H. L. *Organizational Intelligence: Knowledge and Policy in Government and Industry.* New York: Basic Books, 1969.

Cameron Fincher is regents professor and director of the Institute of Higher Education at the University of Georgia. He is associate editor for the AIR of Research in Higher Education *and a Distinguished Member of the Association for Institutional Research.*

Institutional researchers will need increasingly to analyze ill-defined issues that are developing outside the academy. This analysis will require the development of methodologies that anticipate change and an interdisciplinary set of skills that can embrace uncertainty.

Forces Affecting the Future of Postsecondary Education

Richard B. Heydinger

As we consider the future of institutional research, it is important that we recognize the uncertain future of postsecondary education. And indeed, we mean uncertain, not necessarily bleak. As this chapter shows, it is almost as easy to hypothesize an optimistic future for postsecondary education as it is to hypothesize a pessimistic one.

Perhaps at no point in history have so many potentially powerful forces come together to influence the course of postsecondary education in the United States. To cite only a few:

- a declining youth cohort
- an aging faculty
- a rapidly changing technology base that demands unprecedented amounts of new equipment
- a revolution in telecommunications and information systems
- a rapidly decreasing half-life for career obsolescence
- a growing recognition by society of the relationship between economic development and the quality of education and scholarship.

The author gratefully acknowledges the assistance of his colleagues Ann Pflaum and Steven Schomberg in preparing this chapter, as well as the generous support of the W. K. Kellogg Foundation.

Any one of these factors alone could represent a formidable challenge to postsecondary education. When they interact, the dizzying array of alternatives that results can cause even the most confident institutional researcher to consider another line of work.

It almost goes without saying that colleges and universities are loosely coupled organizations (Weick, 1978). History has shown that they, like the Catholic church, are able to bend and adapt to change in ways that practically no other organization can. Colleges and universities also have extremely permeable organizational boundaries. Unlike the proverbial widget factory that is out of touch with contemporary changes, colleges are kept current by their students and by the central role that they play in shaping society's values.

Yet, it is also true that over the centuries colleges and universities have dictated their own pace of change. Because of their flexibility, institutions of higher education have been able to accommodate the demands that society has placed on them without changing much themselves. As Frederick Rudolph (1962, p. 491) has noted, the development of American colleges may be characterized as "drift, reluctant accommodation, belated recognition that while no one was looking, change had in fact taken place." Internal climate and institutional readiness have historically dictated the pace of change in colleges and universities.

These challenges will place new demands on offices of institutional research. The external environment will become a more important variable in efforts to chart the course for our colleges and universities. The methodologies that we have developed for collecting and analyzing data about our internal workings will continue to serve us well. Yet, we must increase our awareness and develop our methodologies for monitoring the external environment. Before I describe some approaches for monitoring external change, I will review some of the forces that could play a significant role in the evolution of postsecondary education.

External Forces with the Potential for Significant Change

This inventory of external forces that have the potential for significant change is necessarily incomplete. One of the hazards in such work is that attempts to examine global forces can reduce them to sweeping generalizations that apply to no one. As Harold Hodgkinson (1983) says, typically no institution falls on the average. Each institution must carefully analyze the external forces in its own context. Only after these forces have been scrutinized and reliable data have been assembled can we begin to discuss the interaction of these trends. The discussion here is a harbinger of the changing nature of the work of institutional researchers. Each section of this inventory ends with a cautionary note calling attention to the major external forces of change.

Demography. No external force has received more attention than our changing demography and rightfully so. It is not necessary for this chapter to recount the shifting population structure of our country. Yet, as policy makers and institutional researchers, we must be careful to separate our own regional and local trends from national statistics. As Harold Hodgkinson (1983) points out, the national decline of 25 percent of the college-going cohort is fiction. The national statistic is comprised of a 40 percent decline in the Northeast — and of no decline in the Sunbelt.

The racial mix of the population is also changing. The baby boom of the 1950s and 1960s saw an upturn in Caucasian births, while the subsequent decline in birthrate has been a downturn in Caucasian births. Throughout this period, the birthrate of minority populations has remained constant (Hodgkinson, 1983). Yet, in some locales the decline in Caucasian births has resulted in a significant increase in the proportion of minority youth. For example, 57 percent of the children in New Mexico are minority. In the near future, the majority of California youth will in fact be minority. The growing percentage of minority youth in the public school systems is already beginning to have an impact. With certainty we can say that across the next twenty years this change in racial mix will place new demands on postsecondary education.

As our population ages, it will also be important for the institutional researcher to study carefully the age mix of the population from which the institution draws. For example, in Minnesota by 1995 the number of people between twenty-five and forty-nine years of age will be 133 percent of what it was in 1980. The increase by more than 400,000 persons in this age group carries significant implications for the economy, demands on social services, and postsecondary education. For the remainder of the twentieth century, the effective institutional researcher will be immersed in the finer details of demography.

Caution: Understand the demographic trends *within the strata and region of the population* from which your institution draws.

Attitudes Toward Postsecondary Education. Although demography is the engine that drives enrollment, the slope of the enrollment curve will be influenced by people's attitudes and reactions to postsecondary education. If jobs are not available for college graduates or if the public becomes disgruntled with the quality of education, the projected enrollment downturn could be accelerated. Yet, America's commitment to the value of education seems strong. In George Gallup's annual survey of public attitudes toward schooling (Gallup, 1984), our educational system was rated as the single most important factor in determining America's future. Americans ranked industrial production and a strong military force well behind the country's educational system in importance. Moreover, 87 percent of all parents with children enrolled in public schools hoped that their children would go on to college. These parents recognized that college offers better job opportunities, higher income, an increased likelihood of being able to cope with the problems encountered in life. Thus, the public's attitude toward the value of postsecondary education remains strong. One can only speculate how quickly this support might erode if a large proportion of college graduates were unable to find meaningful employment. Many observers have predicted that the public may shift its scrutiny of the quality of instruction from elementary and secondary education to today's college population.

Caution: Carefully monitor leading indicators of the public's attitude toward the value placed on receiving a postsecondary degree. Changes in public attitudes will accelerate enrollment trends.

Values That Youth Bring to Our Institutions. If we as institutional researchers are to do a better job of anticipating the forces of change, we must be more systematic in monitoring the changing values of the high school–age population. One of the most comprehensive longitudinal studies has been conducted by Alexander Astin as part of the Cooperative Institutional Research Program at UCLA. Astin's data show that the 1984 freshman class was more materialistic and less altruistic than freshmen of a decade before. Whereas 70 percent of the freshmen in the early 1970s thought that it was important to develop a meaningful philosophy of life, only 45 percent today feel that this is an important objective. As Astin has said, "Making money has become a philosophy of life in itself" (Meyer, 1985, p. 1). In contrast to students of the 1960s and 1970s, today's student body is diverse politically. Overall, students are more conservative; only 14 percent think that college grades should be abolished, and only 26 percent believe that the death penalty should be abolished, yet more than 71 percent feel that being very well off financially is very important.

In general, these statistics do not surprise those who work on college campuses. Yet, the effective office of institutional research will systematically monitor the changing values and expectations of tomorrow's students, for these factors will determine course enrollment behavior and demands for nonacademic support services.

Caution: Study the changing values of high school students, for they represent a large proportion of tomorrow's consumers. Note particularly their reasons for attending college and the expectations and skill levels they bring with them.

Concerns with the Cost of Postsecondary Education. There is growing evidence that the cost incurred by students to attend institutions of postsecondary education will become an issue of paramount importance in the years ahead. Although financial advice columns carry warnings about saving money for college education, most parents do not heed this advice. When children enter college liquid assets are not available to pay the college bills, and the financial aid that is offered is often not enough to cover the total cost.

To balance their own budgets, institutions are raising tuition charges substantially. For example, across an eighteen-month period, tuition at the University of Minnesota rose more than 30 percent. Private colleges almost seem to take pride in who leads the nation as the most expensive. In many states, the tuition increases have been accompanied by increases in financial aid. Yet, regardless of what the statistics say about meeting need, higher costs do limit access. Some professional students are graduating with enormous debt burdens. This encourages them to select the most lucrative specialty within their profession.

Such a trend cannot continue indefinitely. Ultimately, the public may rebel at costs that put postsecondary education out of reach for many in the middle class. Executives of the Washington-based education associations indicate that national policy makers and the media are beginning to take aim at the escalating costs of education. The institutional researcher who is interested in anticipating change will be well served to monitor this growing concern.

Caution: As the cost of postsecondary education begins to disenfranchise certain segments of the population, severe public reactions could result, calling the cost-effectiveness of higher education into question and creating demands for organizational restructuring.

Retraining Needs. As the pace of change quickens, corporations find that their workers quickly become technologically obsolete. As John Bremner (1983, p. 50) has said, "Business training in the next decade will address those whom modern technology will quickly make functionally ignorant if they are not constantly reeducated." People working in the field of training and development can vouch for the burgeoning demand for courses that keep employees current with the most recent developments. Some industries have set up their own training curricula. Often, the variety and number of courses exceed those of a small state university. For example, Westinghouse annually produces a catalogue listing the courses offered in-house that is larger than the catalogues of many universities. Typically, these courses are taught by college professors from nearby institutions.

Individuals no longer think of themselves as pursuing a single career. Today's college graduate will have not one but more likely two, three, or even four careers. Thus, the traditional pattern of schooling, followed by work, followed by leisure in the form of retirement is breaking down. Work, leisure, and education are increasingly intermixed as healthy people with long life spans balance the many challenges and stages of their lives.

The eventual influence of the retraining factor on enrollment in traditional colleges and universities will be strongly influenced by the policies for student aid that support the returning student. A change in financial aid policies, either through the federal government or the personnel policies of private corporations, might significantly increase the proportion of older students who enroll in traditional postsecondary institutions. Currently, it is difficult for most adults to receive the level of support that they need in order to be more than limited part-time students. However, the need for support has been recognized by labor unions and legislators. Legislation has been introduced in recent sessions of Congress that would markedly change the training of today's workers. Programs in the more progressive countries in Europe may be harbingers of the support that the American citizen will receive in order to return to postsecondary education.

Although financial aid policies will be a prime determinant in enrolling the returning adult, perhaps an even greater determinant will be the convenience of the learning situation. Classes that are offered at times and in locations that are convenient to students will attract older students as they attempt to balance the many demands on their lives.

Regardless of the type of instruction taken or the number of older students enrolled, we can rest assured that these students will be self-confident, demand a high-quality education, and expect support services that meet their needs. Institutional researchers should monitor these developments, for they could markedly change the competitive market for postsecondary education.

Caution: Carefully study the retraining patterns of the population. Pay particular attention to the development of financial aid programs and corporate policies that support returning students. Note also that these students will bring a different set of demands to the classroom.

Competition from Other Segments of Society. It is now a generally accepted fact that more than 50 percent of postsecondary education in our society takes place outside the traditional college and university. Policy changes may accelerate this trend, relegating the traditional college and university to an increasingly smaller share of the educational market.

With our country's commitment to the importance of education, entrepreneurs are quick to recognize the business opportunities offered by the ability to provide a high-quality, cost-effective education. For-profit organizations, such as the Wang Institute and the Keller Graduate School of Business, are examples of respected, high-quality training in a specialized market niche. Control Data Corporation continues to move ahead in the development of an introductory engineering curriculum that will be available through its PLATO system. Many educators may criticize these developments and argue for traditional forms of education. Like the railroad industry in the 1950s, they can adopt an attitude that refuses to think creatively about the changing marketplace. Or, like the radio industry in response to the introduction of television, they can respond creatively by recognizing the changing demands for postsecondary education. If they do not, the time is ripe for entrepreneurs to move directly into the postsecondary market. A careful reading of the business section of the newspaper today reveals that new companies aimed at tapping the growing educational market are already forming.

Caution: Do not overlook the competition now emerging in the proprietary sector. Understanding and monitoring such developments is essential if institutional researchers are to move their institution to its best strategic position.

Computation, Communications, and Information Systems. We do not have to belabor the many arguments in support of the revolutionary potential that the advances in microtechnologies and communications bring to the world of education. In Chapter Five, Bernard Sheehan presents an interesting conceptual framework with which to examine the implications of computation and communication for institutional research.

Some argue that, just as the steam engine changed the workplace, the computer—as an extension of our personal information-processing capacities—will alter the educational process. If the barriers to the production of high-quality computerized materials can be overcome, the format of education could truly be revolutionized. We may retrieve information differently, solve problems differently, and interact in new time and space dimensions. On a year-to-year basis, the changes that have been predicted will probably occur slowly, yet as we look back across the decades, much more change will have occurred in education due to these changes than we would ever have predicted.

Caution: Remember that the influence of computation and communications is not a foregone conclusion. It has the potential for being the most significant development in the history of education, yet it might be felt more through other forms of education and training than through traditional postsecondary institutions.

The Attractiveness of Faculty Careers. With growing alarm, many colleges and universities are beginning to recognize the difficulty in attracting the best young minds to a faculty career. Young people are dissuaded by the perceived stodginess of institutions, coupled with their inability to offer a compensation package that can compete with private business. Increasingly, it is argued that those involved with research and development in modern industry have all the benefits and none of the drawbacks of those who teach in our major reserach universities. Personally, I think it is too early to gauge the magnitude of this challenge. However, there can be little doubt that this development could be serious. The decline of the elementary and secondary school system over the past two decades may well be attributed to the waning attraction of teaching in our schools for talented youth, especially women. It does not take much imagination to project a similar fate for the professoriate.

Caution: Collect systematic rather than anecdotal data on the attractiveness and holding power of faculty careers. An erosion in the professoriate could lead to many of the developments already witnessed in elementary and secondary education.

Interaction with Other Segments of Society. One outcome of the debate on the future and challenges facing the American economy has been a reawakening of the recognition that education plays an important role in the economic development of a country. With this recognition, however, has come the demand for high-quality education, clearheaded administrative decisions, and the demand for responsiveness. Major research universities, as well as other postsecondary institutions, are joining hands with business and government to establish cooperative ventures of life. Higher education is finding that it must do more than simply meet business at the negotiating table. It is expected that we will be true partners, meeting business and government at least halfway.

In many cases, this development has revitalized our departments and campuses as we embark on truly exciting new ventures. Even though many of the resulting arrangements may be more form than substance, they offer the potential for a new era in postsecondary education. Yet, we will be well served not to forget the philosophical tenets on which our institutions are founded. Although the term *ivory tower* has pejorative connotations, colleges and universities were established to be the conscience of society. We must ask ourselves whether full-fledged partners in cooperative relationships can also be the critics who question the directions that society is taking and offer new food for thought. The next two decades may well mark a fundamental shift in the role that postsecondary education plays in modern society.

Caution: Trace the growing number of interactions with other segments of society, for they are leading indicators of the changing organizational structure of the postsecondary education. They also are leading indicators of the issues that will find their way onto the institution's agenda.

The Role of Government Regulation. Finally, perhaps the most potent force on the horizon is the influence that government places on postsecondary education. Three alternatives seem possible. With the widely advertised downturn of the college-age population, state governments could decide to step in and rationalize postsecondary education. They might move to close selected institutions while using enrollment policies to keep others open. Second, state governments might find that deciding which institutions to close is so politically explosive that legislatures and higher education coordinating commissions are immobilized. In this case, the free market will prevail, and institutions attracting the highest proportion of students will have the greatest financial flexibility. Third, the administrators of postsecondary institutions may decide that it is in their best long-term interests to act decisively and cooperatively in determining their own futures. This may hold off state and federal agencies from interceding.

Although the external forces exerted by state and federal government may come upon us quickly, emerging trends in these directions should be monitored. Although institutional research requires that we count the number of student credit hours and project enrollments, the effective office of institutional research will not lose sight of governmental policies affecting the changing institutional character of postsecondary education.

Caution: Monitor the changing role of governments in the governance of postsecondary education. Ineffective planning and governance could easily lead to intervention during this period of rapid change.

Possible Institutional Adaptations

Given the broad set of interacting factors just outlined, the future of postsecondary education could take an almost infinite number of paths. To capture the multitude of possible futures available, four scenarios will be presented here. They are written in the context of my home institution, the University of Minnesota. Table 1 lays out the variables used in generating these scenarios. Associated with each variable is a set of possible states that it could

Table 1. Inventory of Possible Key Factors for Scenarios

Direct Inputs to Higher Education	Process Factors	External Factors
A. Funds 　Research 　　1. Boom 　　2. New Partnership 　　3. Continual Decline 　State and Local Financial Support 　　1. Enrollment-based Funding 　　2. Maintain the Industry 　　3. Guided Shrinkage 　Private Sources 　　1. Continued Support 　　2. Drastic Decline 　Student Aid 　　1. Restructuring of Sources 　　2. Crisis in Aid B. Facilities 　1. Replacement Schedule 　2. Gradual Erosion 　3. Selective Building C. Enrollment 　1. Youth Reject Schooling 　2. Tooling and Retooling 　3. Avocational Focus D. Faculty 　1. Brain Drain 　2. Stumbling Through 　3. Renewed Vigor	A. Public Policy Regarding Higher Education 　1. Market Mechanism 　2. Guided Shrinkage 　3. Diversity Maintained B. Internal Academic Governance 　1. Traditional Academic Values Reasserted 　2. Collective Bargaining Takes Hold 　3. Management Values Emerge C. Values of Enrolled Students 　1. Student Consumerism 　2. Concern for the Whole Person 　3. Higher Education as Low Priority	A. Economy[a] 　1. Conventional 　2. Volatile 　3. Decline 　4. Bust B. Computation and Communication 　1. Steady Growth 　2. Explosion 　3. Two-Tiered Access C. Program Demand 　1. All High Tech 　2. Selective Vocational Fields 　3. Natural Resource Crisis 　4. The Bastion of Culture D. Societal Reaction to Higher Education 　1. Greatest Asset 　2. Out-of-touch 　3. Selective Appreciation E. Competition from Other Segments of Postsecondary Education 　1. Little Change 　2. In-House Industrial Programs 　3. Proprietary Boom F. Regulatory Climate 　1. Still Greater Regulation 　2. Reaganism Takes Hold

[a] Premises taken from Hawken and others, 1982.

Source: Heydinger and Zentner, 1983.

assume. (Portions of these scenarios appear in Heydinger and Zentner, 1983, and Heydinger, 1984.)

The first scenario is dubbed "The Official Future." Subconsciously, most organizations and industries adopt the future that they feel is most likely to evolve (Hawken and others, 1982). Such a future becomes commonly accepted wisdom, almost as if it were a fait accompli. This occurs even though we all agree that the future is indeed uncertain.

The Official Future

The course that the university imagined for itself in the early 1980s has been followed. The large base of high-technology industries in Minnesota has continued to expand at a modest rate. New jobs have been created in the Iron Range through an aggressive state-supported program of technology transfer with the university as the mainstay.

After much debate in the 1980s about the best approach for dealing with enrollment, the state legislature adopted a policy of letting the market determine which institutions would thrive and which would fail. Today, institutions in the state chart their own course through aggressive student-recruiting programs, strategic planning, and careful fiscal control.

Although lifelong learning has offset a portion of the projected enrollment downturn, the part-time student population has not been large enough to counteract the decline in the number of young people. With employment opportunities limited, each passing year witnesses students approaching their studies with even more seriousness than the previous year. Today, students are outspoken in their demand for high-quality instruction and up-to-date facilities, for they realize that a postsecondary degree is still the calling card securing meaningful employment.

Support for research programs has been good in selected high-tech areas. Cooperative research organizations and jointly held patents are commonplace for the university. Campus governance is a curious mixture of strategic management (used in developing high-tech and business-oriented programs) and traditional academic governance (still used in the humanities and social science disciplines).

History may in fact show that the cautious outlook expressed in this scenario may give way to a more optimistic future in which postsecondary education becomes an integral part of efforts to assist persons and corporations to cope with a new economic structure. Industry and individuals look to postsecondary education as a means for tooling and retooling. The second scenario expresses this more optimistic future.

Tooling and Retooling

Rather than being boom or bust, the economy has been boom and bust, with businesses in the information and service sectors having more job openings than candidates. Manufacturing has continued to decline.

Both industry and students continue to recognize that a college education is the best road to success. For high school graduates, a college degree will not guarantee a job; however, without a college degree there is no chance of being employed. The unforeseen event in the past decade was the National Retraining Act. This federal legislation, which provides support for workers over age thirty-five to return for retooling, has had a major impact on enrollment at the university. Because of those seeking to retool for a career change, the feared enrollment decline never materialized. As a result, the composition of our student body has undergone fundamental and dramatic shifts. Rather than an enrollment graph that is spiked around the ages of eighteen to twenty-five, a graph of university students is now nearly rectangular across the ages of eighteen to forty-five.

With the increasing proportion of older students, the passive acceptance of poor teaching has become a relic of the past. Students know that their marketability depends on high-quality training on the latest equipment. Thus, lawsuits by students over the misrepresentation of a costly economic good have become commonplace. Faculty members are under increased pressure to offer stimulating and up-to-date classroom material. Because of the greater age span among students, a wide range of values is debated in classroom discussions. As a result, classroom interaction has become more heated.

This more optimistic scenario based on our burgeoning needs to retool could instead be replaced by an extremely pessimistic outlook, in which students perceived little value in attending institutions of postsecondary education. Because there are few jobs and because colleges and universities have done little to bring their pedagogy up to date, youth reject schooling as a valuable pursuit.

Youth Reject Schooling

Despite all efforts by both private and public sectors, the United States has continued to slip as an economic and industrial power. The economy continues to drift as structural unemployment has remained. Some industries continue to expand; job openings are prevalent in selected high-tech areas and in selected skilled trades. The expectations of a micromillenium have generally been realized; computing and communications now play a significant role in people's personal and professional lives. Entertainment and business software is found in every home and office.

Working in concert, these trends have led to a situation of grave concern for the university. It is obvious that all but the most elite youth are rejecting formal education. Although all white-collar jobs require a college credential, there is little job turnover. Thus, there is little motivation to enroll, because one can expect to earn no more than one can in a manual labor position. Youth are outspoken in their criticism of the poor pedagogical technique used in all aspects of formal schooling, whether it be in the high school classroom or the college course. Today's youth have been raised on a steady diet of fast-paced information presented in short bursts. They are accustomed to instant feedback, and they have learned how to handle inputs from a variety of stimuli simultaneously. The format of a college course that has changed little over the past century seems archaic to them.

The impact of these trends has been exacerbated by the high cost of postsecondary education. With the sluggish economy and public opinion swinging against the university, it has slipped on the fiscal agenda of the state. The structure of the university is being threatened as professional schools are threatening to break away and become independent.

From these three quite logical alternatives, we can envision a less likely but nonetheless possible future in which the forces for change interact to create a new industry.

A New Industry Is Born

Many of the changes hoped for in the economy have taken place, and the results for postsecondary education are nothing short of revolutionary. The economy has regained some of its lost momentum as the fundamental move from manufacturing to postindustrial activities begins to shake down. The entrepreneurial spirit in the country continues to burgeon as both policy makers and individuals recognize that innovative activity holds the key to America's future success. The economy is volatile, marked by spurts of growth followed by double-digit inflation. Both federal and local government have created policies to foster new businesses in the hope that this will create long-term, steady growth. The predicted revolution in computing and telecommunications has had a far greater impact on business, education, and home life than all but the boldest predictions envisioned.

Skills are viewed as the key to vocational success, and the education of the whole person has been deemphasized. Given the rapid pace of change, people now expect that they will have three, four, or even five different careers in their working lifetime.

Public officials have recognized the long-term importance for this country of maintaining a viable postsecondary industry. Thus, students have been given adequate financial support to attend the institution of their choice. Some states have instituted taxing policies that tax a family from the birth of a child on so that funds for financial aid will be available throughout the child's life.

All these trends have led to a fundamental reorientation in society's outlook on postsecondary education. Skills, not degrees, are viewed as the most important outcome of an education. With the entrepreneurial spirit sweeping the country, individual entrepreneurs recognize the possibility of establishing proprietary institutions. These ventures do not garner large profits, but they have been viewed as making important contributions to economic development. Hence, there has been a recent explosion of new forms of postsecondary education. Faculty members have set up professionally oriented training programs. Private corporations have established larger, more comprehensive programs. Even the single individual who is highly skilled and an effective teacher has hung out a shingle to offer education. All these developments have become possible because employers look to demonstrable skills rather than to accredited credentials.

If these four scenarios do in fact encompass the broad range of futures for higher education, how does an office of institutional research establish an effective research program? Obviously, we must continue to maintain our internal, institutional data. Yet, at the same time we must develop methodologies that can be used to monitor the external forces that will have a direct bearing on the future of our institutions. The last two sections of this chapter suggest some approaches for addressing this challenge.

Incorporating Environmental Information into Planning and Institutional Research

The three approaches described in this section reach outside colleges and universities to collect information about the external environment. By systematically incorporating such information into the planning process, we are expanding the range of alternatives that the institution can consider as it weighs its future while simultaneously reducing the likelihood that our college or university will be surprised by events and trends of the future. While we recognize the growing uncertainty of the contemporary world, we are consciously attempting to reduce the probability that the world will present us with conditions that we have not previously considered. We are attempting neither to predict the world nor to control it. Instead, we recognize that our institutions of higher education are part of the external world, and we are managing our own destiny within this world.

To incorporate information about the external environment, it is essential, first, to survey the landscape for developments that will have an impact on our college or university. This survey must use a wide-angle lens that brings the trends and developments that could possibly have an impact into focus. This technique is termed *environmental scanning*. Second, as we uncover issues that could influence our institution either positively or negatively, we may choose to act in anticipation of these issues. This technique is termed *issues management*. Third, since the future is uncertain, we may choose to construct a set of plausible futures that will help our institution to think through the many possibilities that it faces. This technique is termed *multiple scenario analysis*.

All three techniques are more art than science. There is no single best way of conducting any of these processes. The most important thing about these approaches is that they raise the consciousness of the institution regarding environmental changes and that they introduce uncertainty into the planning process.

Environmental Scanning. Environmental scanning can be likened to a radar system that moves across all 360 degrees of the horizon looking for trends and events that could have an impact on our institution. In so doing, we should not limit ourselves to trends that will have an immediate and direct bearing on the institution, such as projected shifts in enrollment. Environmental scanning should also consider longer-range, less precise factors that have implications for the future of our institutions, such as teenagers' changing values, the perceived value of higher education, and the growing protest over the use of animals for research. After an issue has been identified as potentially important, it can then be monitored.

The most common approach to environmental scanning is to design a systematic reading program. Typically, corporations involve a diverse group of broad thinkers who are interested in exploring the dimensions of the future and their possible impact on the organization. Care is taken to ensure that the publications being scanned represent a cross section of viewpoints and topics.

The reading group may forward either abstracts or articles to a steering committee, which then discusses the items and decides on the most appropriate next steps. These steps can range from immediate action to a conscious decision to ignore the issue. The reading group is often the discussion group. More detail on this approach can be found in Morrison and others (1983). Many major corporations have assigned the responsibility for monitoring the environment for critical developments to some person or office. At the University of Minnesota, we have formed a group called the Experimental Team on External Assessment, and we are in the initial stages of establishing a scanning program (Hearn and Heydinger, in press).

Once an issue has been deemed important enough to track, a white paper that investigates the topic in detail can be commissioned. This paper can take the form of a research study that collects comprehensive data on the topic, or it can be a thorough synopsis that discusses alternative outlooks and possibilities. With the wealth of faculty expertise available on campuses, these papers can be authored by authorities on the topic. At the University of Minnesota, we commissioned the dean of the Graduate School to author a paper entitled "The Development and Advancement of Knowledge" that examines the disciplines most likely to experience significant change over the next twenty years, and we asked a leading faculty expert on the state's economic climate to author a paper on the Minnesota economy in the year 2000. Both papers provide detailed treatments of important environmental variables; they can be used in a variety of ways to inform and support the planning process.

As stated earlier, environmental scanning is more art than science. Our early experiences at Minnesota indicate that the first attempts to integrate information from disparate sources into a coherent set of issues are both difficult and frustrating. We have spent significant amounts of time debating the purposes of our group and in methodological discussions. We have discussed whether to establish our own formal reading program or to conduct interviews with those who are well informed and who collectively represent a broad section of the university's environment. Overall, the particular methodology that the group selects is not as critical as establishing the discipline of a regularly scheduled activity that scans the environment. The people selected must be broad, integrative thinkers. Bringing such a group together regularly to focus on the environment may be the most critical step in establishing an effective scanning effort.

Issues Management. Once issues have been identified and there is agreement within the institution that a particular issue could have significant impact, the issue can then be managed. Issues management, as the practice has come to be called by its devotees, is the newest in a long line of approaches for coping with the environment. To manage an issue, key questions are asked about the probability of its developing, its likely consequences throughout the institution, and the time frame in which it is likely to develop, that is, near-term, medium-term, or long-term. Recent work by Ian Wilson of SRI and William Renfro of Policy Analysis, Incorporated, lays out four stages in the development of an issue. As Wilson (Foresight Task Force, 1983, p. 22) has said, "the societal concerns of yesterday (stage 1) become the political issues of today (stage 2), the legislated requirements of tomorrow (stage 3), and the litigated penalties of the day after (stage 4)."

The nation's recent concern for the quality of elementary and secondary education is a vivid example. Societal concerns were obviously present (stage 1), but it took the *Nation at Risk* report (National Commission on Excellence in Education, 1983) to articulate these concerns. Today, it is clear that education has become a key political issue (stage 2), since states are introducing legislation (stage 3) on quality measures. Can there be little doubt that regulation and litigation (stage 4) are far behind?

Issues management, like environmental scanning, is more art than science. It combines public relations acumen with strategic planning. It assumes that to be forewarned is to be forearmed. Institutions can turn issues into opportunities if they are abreast of societal developments. One example often cited is the experience of Kaiser Aluminum. When the firm was confronted with the fact that aluminum cans would not easily decompose, it responded by riding the crest of the country's recycling movement to set up recycling centers for its cans.

Once an issue has been identified, it is up to the institution to decide on the best approach for managing it. Case studies from private industry describe the formation of issue teams with a variety of expertise that are pulled together to propose strategies for senior-level management. The word *management* has some pejorative connotations. Hence, issues management can carry the connotation that an institution should manipulate or block the issues that are unfavorable to it. Although the cynical interpretation can always be made, the approach should be viewed in a more favorable light. Issues management rests on the maxim that problems can become opportunities, particularly if the institution has advance warning and time to think through its most constructive response. Moreover, all issues are not a threat to the institution. Some may support the strategic plan of a college or university, and their development should be used to further the strategic ends of the institution.

Multiple Scenario Analysis. The use of scenarios provides one tool for folding information collected through environmental scanning and issues management into the planning process. Just as the scenarios outlined earlier were intended to demonstrate the variety of possible futures that face postsecondary education, scenarios can be used at the institutional level to inform the institution of the many possibilities with which the environment might present us. Generally, planning processes consider only events that are both highly likely and highly important to our institution. Consciously or subconsciously, we ignore issues and events that have a low probability of occurring but that could nonetheless have a major impact on the future of our institution.

Scenarios can be defined as "a comprehensive, internally consistent narrative describing a variety of plausible futures. Usually, they are based on assumptions concerning complex interactions among the international, regional, domestic and/or local social, economic, political, and technological influences" (Foresight Task Force, 1983, p. 7). Scenarios provide integrated mental maps of the future. They weave together trends and possible events from many societal components that might come to influence the future environment of the institution. Scenarios can be used to integrate the insights gained from environmental scanning. They require the scenario authors to ask themselves how a trend in one seemingly isolated segment of the environment may be related to other trends. Perhaps most important, they communicate to the reader that the future is fundamentally uncertain; we cannot predict the events of tomorrow.

Scenarios are used to set the context for planning. When they are distributed as background information for another formal cycle of planning, they inform the recipients of possible environmental trends and events that might affect the future of their own department or college. These environmental factors are thus more likely to be folded into the planning process. Central administration can take this process a step further by indicating that unit plans will be tested against the scenarios. By considering multiple futures, we can test the robustness of our strategies to see how they fare in a variety of settings.

Space does not permit me to discuss the construction of scenarios. Such a discussion can be found in Heydinger and Zentner (1983) and in other sources that are not focused on education. Suffice it to say that scenarios can take a variety of forms, ranging from a short paragraph (as in this chapter) to a thirty-page essay (Hawken and others, 1982), from descriptions to numerical tables. Like the other techniques described here, the construction of scenarios is more art than science. It requires a thorough understanding of the current trends and future forces affecting the development of our society. Scenarios for institutional planning require more focus on environmental variables, more specificity, and in most cases a more regional or local focus than the examples in this chapter display.

As postsecondary education moves into an era of strategic choice, systematic information on external trends and events will be just as important as detailed operational information. Although people have recognized this in the past, little systematic work has been done to investigate the most effective and most efficient methods for collecting such information. To date, the business world has had modest success with the three methodologies just described. Although there is no certainty about the types of external information that will be needed in the future to support strategic planning and institutional research, we can speculate on how these demands will change the skills needed for institutional research across the next two decades.

Skills Needed for Institutional Research

This section argues that, if an office of institutional research is to be effective in the future, the set of skills required will be broader than that typically used today. Detailed institutional data will be important, and the capacity to separate accurate operational data from misleading statistics will always be of paramount importance. As in any maturing profession, the techniques needed to master these basic skills are known.

Across the next two decades, institutional researchers will increasingly need to trace broad and ill-defined issues as they develop within our society. The next stage in the evolution of institutional research calls for the capacity to trace and anticipate significant changes in our particular environment. The development of such a capacity requires an office of institutional research to develop some new capabilities and sensitivities.

A different disciplinary background will be needed. To date, institutional research has rested primarily on the techniques of survey research, the approaches of economics, expertise in quantitative manipulation, and a familiarity with public policy analysis. Increasingly, the skills of anthropology, geography, sociology, and political science will be needed. These disciplines have developed a perspective and methodologies that facilitate the analysis of complex societal phenomena. They have a perspective that asks the researcher to stand back and grasp the interplay of diverse social phenomena.

Yet perhaps more important, the office of institutional research will need to be able to bring an interdisciplinary perspective to bear on its analysis. For example, the teams at Shell Oil Company that develop its planning scenarios consist of a lawyer, an engineer, an economist, an accountant, and a political scientist. Just as we argue for the importance of the liberally educated person, institutional research will require a broad set of skills.

To trace the development of external issues, institutional researchers will need to become familiar with a broad set of data bases. For example, recent concern with enrollment projections had led institutional research offices to become intimately familiar with census data and other demographic data bases. Such documents as the *United States Statistical Abstract,* public opinion polls, and the journal *American Demographics* will become necessities of effective institutional research.

In allocating the scarce human resources of an office of institutional research, we must resist the temptation to refine existing methodologies, such as enrollment projection models. Instead, we must be willing to tackle the larger questions. In a rapidly changing world marked by fundamental shifts, decision makers will not pay for highly refined operational data. Instead, they will desire anticipatory signals that will keep them from being surprised. In this milieu, rigorously defining a complex issue may bring as much enlightment as collecting data about it. If institutional research is to be effective in this turbulent period, we must not bury ourselves in operational data but instead guarantee that we are investigating the fundamental questions that will determine the future of our institutions. Having delineated these questions, we must be willing to conduct exploratory research that will require all the skills of a broad, liberal education.

Thus, the next step in the evolution of institutional research will require broad, integrative skills. Although the skills needed to conduct a rigorous analytical study will not lose their importance, they will be joined by a need to interpret broad societal phenomena in a context specific to the future of our own institution. In comparison with debates on the definition of teaching load, a discussion focused on a potentially important societal trend will seem at best ambiguous and at worst frustrating. The number cruncher, whether human or machine, will still play an important role. However, that role will be shared by the broad integrative thinker who can see through seemingly unrelated tidbits of information to anticipate the emerging issue for an institution. Great leaders and entrepreneurs have always had this knack. Offices of institutional research will have to possess it if they are to realize their full potential in assisting institutional policy makers.

References

Bremner, J. E. "Dawning Need: Perpetual Retraining." *Financier,* September 1983, pp. 48-51.
Foresight Task Force. "Foresight in the Private Sector: How Can Government Use It?" Report submitted to Ralph C. Bledsoe, Special Assistant to the President, January 1983.
Gallup, G. W. "Poll of the Public's Attitude Toward the Public Schools." *Standard Education Almanac, 1983-84.* Chicago: Marquis, 1984.
Hawken, P., Ogilvy, J., and Schwartz, P. *Seven Tomorrows.* Toronto: Bantam Books, 1982.
Hearn, J. C., and Heydinger, R. B. "Scanning the External Environment of a University: Objectives, Constraints, and Possibilities." *Journal of Higher Education,* in press.
Heydinger, R. B. "Using External Information in Planning." In M. Waggoner, R. Alfred, and M. Peterson (Eds.), *Academic Renewal: Advancing Higher Education Toward the Nineties.* Ann Arbor: University of Michigan, 1984.
Heydinger, R. B., and Zentner, R. "Multiple Scenario Analysis: Introducing Uncertainty into the Planning Process." In J. L. Morrison, W. L. Renfro, and W. I. Boucher (Eds.), *Applying Methods and Techniques of Futures Research.* New Directions for Institutional Research, no. 39. San Francisco: Jossey-Bass, 1983.
Hodgkinson, H. Unpublished presentation to the Minnesota Governor's Commission on the Future of Postsecondary Education, St. Paul, June 20, 1983.
Meyer, T. J. "Freshman Are Materialistic but Not Conservative, Study Finds; Poll Shows GOP Winning Students." *Chronicle of Higher Education,* January 16, 1985, p. 1.
Morrison, J. L., Renfro, W. L., and Boucher, W. I. (Eds.). *Applying Methods and Techniques of Futures Research.* New Directions for Institutional Research, no. 39. San Francisco: Jossey-Bass, 1983.
National Commission on Excellence in Education. *A Nation at Risk: The Imperative for Educational Reform.* Washington, D.C.: United States Department of Education, April 1983.
Reichard, D. J. "Commission to Reassess the Purposes and Objectives of the Association of Institutional Relations." Unpublished working paper, University of North Carolina at Greensboro, n.d.
Rudolph, F. *The American College and University.* New York: Knopf, 1962.
Weick, K. "Educational Organizations as Loosely Coupled Systems." *Administrative Science Quarterly,* 1978, *23,* 541-552.

Richard B. Heydinger is an assistant vice-president for academic affairs at the University of Minnesota. He is a member of the AIR executive committee and chairs the Professional Development Services Board.

External trends, new technology, and emerging organizational theories are changing institutional governance and management. These changes in governance and management will affect the character of institutional research.

Changing Governance and Management Strategies

Frank Schmidtlein

The governance and management processes in colleges and universities depend to some extent, as Fincher notes in Chapter Two, on data, their analysis and interpretation, and periodic policy studies that typically are provided by institutional research offices. The institutional research data, analyses, and studies help to shape the agenda of governance and management processes. however, the effect is reciprocal. Institutional research agendas are in turn shaped by the forces that institutional governance and management processes confront. This effect is undoubtedly much greater than the effect of institutional research on governance and management. Consequently, changes in the governance and management strategies of colleges and universities that result from external and internal forces will have an important influence on the future character and content of institutional research. This chapter examines some changes affecting institutions, their implications for governance and management, and the implications of the governance and management changes for institutional research.

Sources of Change

The prediction of change in human endeavors is a risky business. Any cursory review of past predictions by eminent scholars and practitioners about the future character of higher education reveals that they were often wrong.

Nevertheless, all human actions are based on some assumptions about the character of the future, and a great deal of human energy is devoted to discerning probable future conditions. This activity ranges all the way from praying for divine guidance and examining chicken entrails to the rationalistic processes described by Heydinger in Chapter Three.

Social science theories are beginning to provide some structure for examinations of the mechanisms of change. These theories have some potential for improving our predictive powers. Open systems theories of organization, exemplified by Katz and Kahn (1966), imply that changes in institutions result from their need to adapt to changing external conditions, from new technologies, and from new perspectives that evolve from changing theories and new knowledge.

Change Resulting from Adaptations to External Conditions. Open systems theory suggests that a university or college produces some mix of educated students, scholarship and research, and public service. In exchange, society supplies the educational institution with the resources to continue to produce these services. When external events occur that change the value that clients place on the institution's services, that lessen the resources that society is able or willing to make available, or both, then the institution must change if it is to overcome the effects of these events. Otherwise, it will not gain the resources needed, it will be forced to retrench or even close. Governance and management strategies are the means by which an organization attempts to bring about needed changes.

This view of one source of organizational change suggests that, to predict changing governance and management strategies, one must first determine what changes appear to be taking place outside of institutions that require them to make adaptations. Then, an assessment must be made of the implications that these adaptations will have for governance and management strategies. Finally, given our interest in institutional research, we must attempt to predict the consequences that these emerging governance and management strategies will have for the conduct of institutional research.

In Chapter Three of this volume, Heydinger describes many trends affecting the future of higher education and some of the influences that they are apt to have on institutional research. These trends will also cause changes in institutional governance and management emphases and strategies that have implications for institutional research. This chapter explores the connections between these trends, governance and management emphases and strategies, and institutional research. However, change in governance and management strategies can come from another source.

Change Resulting from New Technologies. The term *technologies* refers to the characteristic methods that institutions employ to transform their inputs into outputs, including such procedures as budget protocols as well as hardware and instrumentation. Sheehan, in Chapter Five of this volume, discusses the integration of computer and communications systems into administrative operations. The primary application has been the rapid and cost-effective processing of routine institutional business functions, record-keeping activities, and data collection. A second type of technology is illustrated by so-called rationalistic control and coordination processes, such as management by objectives and zero-based budgeting. A third application combines the first two, making use of the computer to drive specialized and complex interactive programs for academic budgeting and planning.

When institutions discover new technologies that result in operating efficiencies, in theory they gain a competitive advantage. Other institutions must then change their technologies if they are to continue to compete on favorable terms. Higher education is a labor-intensive enterprise and generally has not achieved large efficiencies from new technologies. However, the advent of computers certainly has increased capabilities for conducting research and performing some business and planning functions. Institutional research has benefited particularly from the introduction of new technology. The use of computers and applied mathematics has tended to increase capabilities in most instances, rather than to decrease institutional costs. The governance and management implications of new computer technology are discussed by Sheehan in Chapter Five.

Change Resulting from New Perspectives on the Character of Organizations. In addition to changing external conditions and new technological developments, there is a third impetus to change in governance and management practices. A highly influential book by Kuhn (1962) describes how changing theoretical assumptions or "paradigms" underlying scientific research have revolutionized various fields of inquiry. Over time, theoretical transformations have altered our perceptions of organizations and consequently changed our assumptions about effective governance and management practices. Two such examples were Weber's (Gerth and Mills, 1946) formulation of the concept of bureaucracy and Katz and Kahn's (1966) concept of organizations as open systems.

As new concepts are transmitted to new generations of students and practitioners, theories on organizational behavior, structure, and processes evolve. These new theories lead to new management concepts, techniques, and processes such as PPBS, project management techniques such as PERT, quality circles, and strategic planning. One example of popularizations of new theoretical perspectives that accelerates their translation into practice is the recent book by Peters and Waterman (1982). These authors describe newly emerging organizational theory from which practices of successful businesses were derived or at least with which they are congruent. Such new management techniques typically are adopted in form, if not in substance, by higher education governance and management strategies. Their adoption often affects the focus and intensity of institutional research activities. Thus, this chapter will also examine some implications that developments in organizational behavior theory have for changing governance and management strategies and their consequences for institutional research.

Effects of External Trends

The trends that Heydinger describes in Chapter Three have been described by others, including Glenny (1980), Glenny and Schmidtlein (1983), and Breneman (1979). Some speculation follows on how these trends are likely to affect governance and management strategies and on their implications for institutional research.

Retrenchment and Its Consequences. Retrenchment is the label popularly given to actions that institutions must take when faced with the effects of fewer students, less money, or both. The nature and consequences of retrenchment have been well documented by Mingle and Associates (1981), Hyatt and others (1984), and many others. The demographic and economic conditions creating a need for many institutions to retrench appear likely to persist for at least the next ten years. These trends seem likely to affect governance and management in the ways described in the following paragraphs.

Focus on External Events. The prospect of retrenchment is shifting the attention of many higher education administrators toward the external trends that are the source of their difficulties. Two manifestations of this shift in attention is the recent popularization in higher education of the concepts of strategic planning and marketing. In Chapter Three, Heydinger suggests the techniques of environmental scanning and issues management. The strategic planning concept, described by such authors as Shirley (1982) and Keller (1983), suggests that institutions should aggressively collect data and assess trends that are likely to affect the type and number of students they will attract and their ability to maintain the quality of their programs. Armed with this information, they should determine the nature and extent of the adaptations needed if they are to continue to prosper and to introduce needed changes. It can be hoped that this information will be collected far enough in advance of dramatic developments to permit institutions to anticipate their consequences and to take steps to avoid the disruptions attending an unforeseen crisis. Heydinger describes the process in some detail.

Marketing is another strategy that assesses demographic, economic, and social trends. Institutions examine these trends in the context of their market share of students, and the resulting information is used to determine where the competitive advantages lies. With this knowledge of the marketplace, an institution can assess its competitive advantages and change its programs, if necessary, to concentrate efforts in areas where it has the greatest comparative advantage. Finally, it devises recruitment strategies that attract students from the market segment targeted for recruitment. Marketing plans are basically a subset of the contents of a broader strategic plan.

There is some argument over whether specific, formalized strategic planning and marketing processes are passing fads, like so many of the other innovations that higher education has adopted from business and government. For example, General Electric recently moved away from the strategic planning processes that it had employed. There is no doubt, however, that the circumstances that are causing attention to be paid to external trends will persist. Institutions will have strong incentives to obtain and assess external trend data. Governance and management strategies will be devised to accomplish this task.

These circumstances suggest that, whatever form management strategy takes, institutional research offices will increasingly be called on to provide data and analyses on trends that pose a threat of retrenchment, or at least institutional research will be viewed as useful if it does so. Attention that currently is given to demographic trends when making enrollment projections may be supplemented by examinations of state or regional economic trends that affect family income and government revenues. Developing trends in the financing of other public services that compete with higher education for tax dollars might reveal future problems and lead to strategies for competing more effectively for budget shares. Shifting public preferences and perceptions of higher education are another external factor that merits the attention of institutional researchers. Heydinger suggests some strategies for accomplishing this aim.

The extent to which institutional research offices shift their attention to external trends will depend on the value that campus leaders place on anticipating events and on the returns that they expect from the considerable costs involved in such data gathering and analysis.

Shifts in Location of Decisions. Retrenchment decisions typically are highly controversial and frequently have to be made within severe time constraints. These circumstances seem likely to centralize decision making at top campus levels. Campus faculty, department chairs, and deans are going to find it difficult and unrewarding to take a lead in making decisions on selective cutbacks of resources and programs. Peer relationships become very strained in such circumstances. Consequently, there undoubtedly will be a tendency to allow difficult decisions to drift up to central campus offices. Also, when major retrenchment decisions must be made, there are often very tight deadlines for the taking of action. This situation further limits the opportunity for broad campus responses. An increase in the influence of central campus staff on such vital decisions seems likely to result in faculty demands for clear specifications of the data, processes, and criteria by which decisions are reached.

Since a need for confidentiality and tight time constraints will curtail the more deliberate and extensive consultation typically sought when decisions must be made, administrators are likely to seek more data to justify their decisions, and they will need to describe the processes by which decisions are reached in considerable detail. The time constraints on decisions may cause budget, planning, and institutional research endeavors to be more tightly linked. These circumstances seem likely, therefore, to increase the demand for readily accessible institutional research data and also to increase the prominence of the institutional research function. Data available on short notice in institutional research offices will substitute for the information made available in the past through extensive consultations and participation, which are no longer possible in today's constrained circumstances. Data will be needed to justify the equity and objectivity of retrenchment decisions and to justify conclusions reached under circumstances where the resulting decisions cannot be legitimated through the normal processes of consultation.

In contrast to the tendency within campuses to centralize decision making, state-level and system-level offices are likely to decentralize the decision-making process. The unpleasantness and complexities involved in making retrenchment decisions seem likely to encourage state-level and system-level officials to defer decisions to the campus level. They will lack the detailed information needed to make effective, detailed retrenchment decisions, and they will discover that there are few political rewards for those who reduce or eliminate programs. However, they will be aware of trends and areas where decisions appear to be needed. Consequently, they will seek campus data and press for campus actions. There may be increasing state demands for ad hoc data submissions and for the policy studies needed to monitor institutional responses to the problems they confront. This will be particularly true if legislative staffs or the staffs of other state agencies and systems headquarters continue to increase in size. Institutional research offices will have to supply many of these data.

Development Function Growth. The adverse demographic and economic circumstances confronting institutions today are heightening their interest in private sources of funds. Independent institutions, of course, have historically placed great emphasis on fund raising or, as it is often termed, on campus development. Recently, however, no doubt in response to curtailments of state and local budgets, public institutions have increased their emphasis on development. This increasing effort seems likely to require data and analyses on prospective sources of funds. Data will also be needed on campus characteristics, plans, and priorities in order to sell the necessity for private support of particular initiatives. The extent to which institutional research offices currently serve this purpose is unclear, but it does appear to offer opportunities, if not demands, for future involvement.

Concern with Faculty Vitality. Demographic and economic trends have affected faculty in two ways. First, the demand for new faculty has decreased in most disciplines over the past fifteen years, while the supply has remained high. Consequently, faculty bargaining power has declined in the employment marketplace. Opportunities for advancement have lessened, and average faculty age is increasing. Student interest in majors has changed, and redeployment of faculty in response to these shifts has become more difficult as disciplines with declining enrollments have become tenured in. Second, the softness in the faculty employment market has caused salaries to decline in relation to the cost-of-living index. Low faculty salaries in such fields as engineering and computer science have made it very difficult to recruit quality faculty because of strong demand from business and government, which can offer higher salaries. There is some evidence that many of the brightest undergraduates, who in the past would have gone on to graduate work and sought faculty positions, are now seeking in nonacademic fields. Concern is rising that these factors will lead to an overall decline in faculty quality. Parallels are being drawn with the alleged decline in the quality of elementary and secondary school teachers as the result of low salaries.

This rising concern over the quality of faculty seems likely to continue the attention that institutional research devotes to comparative salary studies. This examination may be broadened to include comparisons with salaries in nonacademic settings where those possessing graduate degrees are employed. More attention is likely to be focused on trends in faculty quality; particularly as faculty hired during the enrollment boom of the 1960s begin to retire and increasing numbers of new faculty are needed to replace them. Analyses of internal reallocations of faculty will continue to be important as student demand for courses in various disciplines creates imbalances in work load. Institutional researchers typically have been sensitive to the need for faculty salary and work load data. This area promises to provide increasing demands for data and analysis in the future.

Need for Campus Management Flexibility. In order to adapt effectively to the changes being forced by retrenchment, campuses will need considerable flexibility if they are to act quickly and creatively. The recent study by Kerr (1984) highlights the constraints affecting the chief executive officers of institutions; Kerr suggests that top administrators need to be given the flexibility to act more forcefully. Some states, such as Colorado, Kentucky, Maryland, and Minnesota, have recognized the need for greater institutional flexibility and acted to lessen the procedural constraints and state controls on their public campuses. This trend, which seems to be gaining momentum, is related to a general movement in our nation toward decentralization and decreased governmental regulation. This movement is typified by the efforts of the current administration to reduce governmental regulations, and it is consistent with the practices of many successful businesses as Peters and Waterman (1982) describe them.

However, this movement toward increased campus flexibility can also be viewed as a threat to achieving adequate public accountability, a concern of considerable magnitude over the past twenty-five years. There is substantial agreement that important public social objectives, such as desegregation, affirmative action, employment equity for women, and consumer protection, can be achieved only through government-imposed accountability processes. In addition, government has always taken an interest in financial accountability.

Elected officials are more secure when they can point to the measures they have installed to ensure that the public trust is not being abused.

Some accommodation will have to be made between the values represented by campus flexibility and the values represented by governmental accountability. At the moment, the trend seems to be moving toward increased flexibility, but its magnitude and persistence are hard to predict. An argument can be made that the autonomy that campuses may attain by being granted more flexibility would reduce external reporting requirements and decrease the work load and prominence of institutional research offices. However, one could also speculate that increased autonomy would increase government's demands for the data needed to evaluate how well that autonomy was being exercised. As for internal demands for data, campus officials may show more interest in data so that they can defend the decisions they will increasingly be called on to make. However, they also may feel less compunction to justify their decisions to external audiences if formal constraints are reduced. In short, the consequences for institutional research are rather unclear at this time. However, institutional researchers will undoubtedly be called on to help justify the benefits provided by increased flexibility.

Search for New Approaches to Justify Budgets. The major basis for justifying campus budget increases has traditionally been increased enrollments, measured in terms of full-time equivalent (FTE) students. Qualitative appeals and special situations have been exploited for increases, but the resulting increases were usually specific to particular situations and generally not substantial.

The decline in the number of potential students in most states is generating a search for new ways of justifying budget increases. Half way into the 1980s, quality is replacing access as the rallying cry of higher education. Tennessee has experimented with techniques providing institutions with money on the basis of performance measures. Higher education links to economic development are being used to obtain funds. There is a growing body of literature on organizational effectiveness and renewed interest in outcome measurement. The hope continues that demonstrations that desired outcomes have been achieved will provide a new basis for budget appeals.

The economic constraints affecting most states make it unlikely that budgetary links to FTE students will be loosened very much during enrollment declines, although there may be some recognition of the increasing unit costs that occur during retrenchment. Measurement of outcomes presents formidable problems. Therefore, while institutional researchers are likely to be involved in some efforts to find and support new ways of justifying increased resources, their efforts are apt to be intermittent and inconclusive. The search for quality measures is unlikely to alter either traditional budget justifications or institutional research participation in budgeting. Some new kinds of information may be included in budget justifications, but the major basis for decisions will remain FTE students, whose number measures the primary instructional work load of institutions. The interest in outcome measurement seems likely to rise briefly as its possibilities are explored and then to wane as the problems inherent in the use of such measures become apparent. The recent report by the Study Group on the Conditions of Excellence in American Higher Education (1984) seems likely to be a vehicle for promoting a debate over the feasibility and desirability of outcome measurement in higher education.

One successful strategy for increasing budgets, as already noted, is to link higher education with economic growth. Institutions are currently exploiting their role in promoting the expansion of high-technology industry by getting increased funding for their engineering, computer science, and related programs. They are establishing technology research centers and emphasizing training for high-tech careers. Institutional research offices have an opportunity to collect and analyze data on the performance of these efforts that will be useful for institutional assessment and budget justification. Studies have been made of the economic impact of institutions on their communities, but little information seems to have been developed on the character and results of institutions' links to business and industry in their region.

Concerns with Administrative Costs. When retrenchment becomes necessary, a campus begins a search to identify areas of lowest priority for shrinkage or elimination and areas most vulnerable to reductions. These two bases for budget cuts do not necessarily target the same areas. Current evidence suggests that retrenchment perceived as temporary and as having a modest impact usually results primarily in across-the-board percentage budget cuts. When retrenchment is more severe and persistent, then selective cuts are more likely to occur.

The survival of institutional research in this environment seems likely to hinge on whether it is viewed as a vital tool for making wise decisions on critical issues or as expendable administrative overhead. The institutional research office must have both an important and a visible role in campus decisions, and it needs the support of influential campus constituencies if it is to weather severe cuts in campus budgets. The most likely scenario, given the important uses of institutional research described in various parts of this volume, is that some institutional research offices will suffer cuts, a few will be eliminated (at least as a central campus function), and many will survive relatively intact. The outcome will be affected by the perspectives of campus leaders, by the campus political support that the institutional research office enjoys, and by its record of staff skill and productivity. When institutional research offices are eliminated, they are likely before too long to reappear or find their functions incorporated into some other office. While the role of data and analysis does not have the primacy that some suggest is needed for achieving effective management, it is too important not to be pursued by institutions, given the demands for data and planning that they now confront.

Growth of Student Financial Aid and Its Consequences. Other trends besides retrenchment have implications for institutional research. The amounts of money devoted to student financial aid have increased markedly over the past fifteen years. These increases have occurred at state and institutional as well as at federal levels. Data collection and research on the effects and distribution of this aid have not kept pace with its growth.

The great economic significance of student financial aid seems likely to focus institutional research attention on data collection and analysis in this area. In the short run, federal attempts to restrict or reduce the amount of funds devoted to student aid will lead to efforts to collect and assess data that can be used to identify the effects of actions to reduce and to justify the need for continued support. At many campuses, data on student aid are not as extensive or as systematically kept as are data on enrollments or degrees earned. The federal government and states by and large have not provided an incentive to establish sophisticated institutional financial aid data bases by requesting data as detailed as they collect on enrollment. The inadequacy of the data available on student financial aid seems likely to be increasingly recognized. Improvements probably will have to be initiated at the campus level, since practices are complex and diverse, and data gathering and analysis are extremely difficult. Institutional research offices seem likely to play a major role in any efforts to improve and analyze student aid data. They could serve as a catalyst to improve student financial aid data as well as merely to collect such data. All this argues that institutions will find it in their self-interest to continue and expand the data collection and analysis that they have been doing in this area.

Concern with Equity and Increases in Litigation. The general growth of litigation in our society has not bypassed higher education. The legal staffs employed to handle campus problems have grown larger, and they have required data and studies to defend campuses in many types of cases. Federal and state legislation and regulations concerning equity have had a major impact on institutional requirements for data collection and analysis. Despite the questions now being raised about the philosophy and effectiveness of these laws and regulations, the data systems and studies that they have instigated seem likely to persist. The basic problems that these systems and studies address have not disappeared. The data systems are largely in place, and they are costly to modify. Expectations are well established for the data that they provide. When litigation arises, it typically requires substantial data collection and analysis efforts. After the case begins it is too late to collect much of the relevant data. Institutional research offices frequently are called on to supply these data and studies. All this argues that institutions will find it in their self-interest to continue most of the data collection and analysis that they have been doing in this area.

There is some speculation that a conservative trend in the nation may reduce the government's interest in equity and that increasingly conservative judicial decisions could lessen the prospects for success in some types of litigation, thus reducing current incentives to bring lawsuits against institutions. There is very little evidence to support this speculation at present. The role of institutional research in this area seems likely to continue to be important for some time to come. In fact, if the interest of institutional researchers in research needed to support litigation continues to grow, as the increase in sessions dealing with this subject at the AIR forums seems to show, the work load in this area may increase rather than diminish over the next few years.

Effects of the Microcomputer Revolution. The implications of the explosive increase in the numbers of microcomputers on college campuses is discussed by Sheehan in Chapter Five of this volume. Tetlow (1984) discusses the use of microcomputers for planning and management support. The decentralization of computing and the growth of small, independent data bases seem certain to present formidable challenges for campuses. Problems in the consistency of data reporting, in the definition of data elements, in the consistency of data base design, and in the coordination of data systems development in a decentralized environment will have to be resolved.

As major consumers of data and typically as the coordinating point for external reports, institutional research offices will have to become involved in these problems. In fact, they could be one of the major actors, if not the major actor. They are in a position to mediate some of the technical and policy disputes that are certain to arise.

Effects of New Perspectives on the Character of Organizations

Institutional researchers, either implicitly or explicitly, operate on the basis of the theoretical assumptions that they hold about organizational behavior. The extent to which their advice is heeded and to which their efforts contribute to policy and decisions largely depends on whether their assumptions correspond to institutional realities and to the assumptions that campus leaders hold about those realities. If, over time, institutional researchers' theoretical perspectives on organizational issues make their advice and products irrelevant, then their role will be diminished. Similarly, if their theoretical assumptions are significantly different from those of the campus leadership, then leaders will tend to ignore their advice whatever its intrinsic value. Consequently, the continuing success of institutional researchers demands that they be sensitive to emerging theories and norms of institutional behavior as well as to the theories and norms held by their constituencies.

Considerable risk is involved in predicting the evolution of organizational theory and its implications. One is apt to mistake contemporary fads for more fundamental long-term conceptual shifts and to assume that one's own notions represent the leading edge of theory. Nevertheless, governance and management theories have critical implications for institutional research practices. Therefore, this section describes some emerging theoretical perspectives that are challenging four commonly held views about organizational behavior. Each of these four views has been considered an element of rational management thinking. Current theoretical perspectives indicate that management thinking may not be as rational as assumed. In addition, this section describes a theoretical perspective on organizational structure that has implications for the location of institutional research.

First, both organizations and units within organizations are commonly viewed as acting rationally when they rely heavily on intelligence derived from research and analysis in making decisions. When modern quantitative techniques for research and analysis are not given prominence, the administrators responsible are often labeled as acting irrationally. This labeling of administrative behavior as irrational is particularly congenial to institutional researchers. After all, their mission is to provide formal research and analysis to aid in decision making. To give legitimacy to other sources of organizational intelligence risks downgrading their own importance.

Second, the effectiveness of decisions is often evaluated on the basis of economic standards of rationality. Institutional research staffs often have training in economics and economic methods of analysis. In addition, economic variables in organizations are typically more susceptible to quantification than many noneconomic variables are. Therefore, institutional researchers typically have a tendency to emphasize the rationality of economic bases for decisions.

Third, the commonly accepted approaches to making organizational decisions presume the presence of organizational goals and view management as designing means to reach these goals. When institutional administrators do not specify clear goals and develop plans to reach them, institutional researchers may question the rationality of their decision-making processes.

Fourth, the issues that organizations confront are often conceived of as problems. These problems are viewed as having solutions. Once solutions have been discovered, they can be applied again in similar situations. An effective organization is one that discovers problems at an early stage and that has the ability to design creative solutions. The data and analyses of institutional researchers help to define problems and provide a basis for the evaluation of solutions.

Current open systems theories of organizational behavior suggest that each of the views just listed is seriously limited in its utility. They are not necessarily the rational way of viewing organizational behavior. The nature of these limitations are described in the paragraphs that follow.

Reliance on Research and Analysis. Contemporary views of proper organizational performance frequently place primary emphasis on data gathering and analysis as a means for gaining organizational intelligence and making wise decisions. The intelligence gained through informal feedback from internal and external constituencies tends to be viewed as unscientific and often as an irrational basis for decisions. The use of informal feedback from past actions in taking limited initiatives and then in making corrections based on consequences is seen as a wasteful process when analysis undertaken prior to initiatives might reveal the proper action. However, data are expensive, many important variables are difficult to quantify, there is often little time for analysis, and predictions are generally uncertain. Consequently, much of the intelligence that organizations use comes from informal evaluations of reactions to past courses of action, not from a priori, systematic analysis of potential courses of action. Therefore, an administrator need not be irrational if he or she places considerable weight on informal feedback from constituencies, given the cost of formal data collection and analysis.

Recognition that the information on which decisions rest comes from daily organizational interactions perhaps more than it does from data and analysis should not be interpreted as downgrading the role of institutional research. It merely clarifies the constraints within which useful data collection and analysis take place. Ideally, the more one knows about the characteristics of an institution's environment and its internal conditions through such data and research, the better equipped one is to make effective decisions. However, an institutional researcher can better support decisions when he or she is sensitive to the costs, time constraints, and limits on quantification that affect research. Such sensitivity can help to guide efforts to areas where research can be most timely and relevant to decisions. Similarly, such sensitivity can help an institutional researcher to appreciate the broad intelligence that administrators obtain from their daily interactions and from feedback regarding past actions. Institutional research can be viewed as complementing, not supplanting, other important sources of institutional intelligence.

The sensitivity to the value of different sources of intelligence must be reciprocal. Institutional administrators must share with institutional researchers intelligence from other sources that is relevant to the issues that institutional research staffs address. Otherwise, institutional research staffs will find it difficult to present data and analyses that are fully relevant to the issues being addressed. Institutional research staffs cannot be expected to be most helpful if they cannot shape their priorities and analyses in the light of other sources of organizational intelligence.

Use of Economic Standards of Effectiveness. Economic standards of rationality are often emphasized in evaluations of organizational decisions. Consequently, the range of resources involved in organizational exchanges is often much too narrowly defined. At least four classes of resources are exchanged in the organizational marketplace: economic goods and services, social assets, human qualities and skills, and information. The value placed on particular resources when making a decision varies with the circumstances. Often, a political resource or a cultural value may outweigh a primarily economic efficiency concern.

The first resource, economic goods and services, is the most common focus of policy attention. The rules of exchange for economic resources are more highly formulated than the rules for exchange of other kinds of resources. Economic data are generally more readily available for analysis than data on other kinds of resources are.

The second class of resources is social assets, such as status, legitimacy, authority, political power, association with core cultural values, and constituent loyalty. Little attention has been focused on these assets as a form of organizational resource. Homans (1961), Blau (1964) and Ilchman and Uphoff (1971), among others, have developed some exchange theories of social resources. Social resources are hard to measure and quantify so they commonly are neglected in formal modes of policy analysis. Yet, they are of great importance to the calculations of perceptive administrators, and they are given significant weight when arriving at decisions.

The third class of resources is human skills and qualities. These resources also are difficult to analyze and quantify, but experienced administrators know that their organization is no better than the people whom they employ. Difficult choices are required when determining how much an outstanding person is worth to an organization, because a salary based on pure merit can raise equity concerns among other employees and create offsetting costs in organizational morale. Sometimes a budget action based on economic considerations can cause the most competent persons to leave the organization, which costs it more in overall terms than the budget action saves.

The fourth class of resources is information. Just as in the case of social assets, people often fail to realize that information is exchanged and employed in ways designed to enhance the net advantages of persons and organizations. The phenomenon is often noted of the bureaucrat who, in order to protect his position from ambitious subordinates, does not allow them to obtain a full view of operations and discussions in progress. When individuals do not fully divulge information, there is a tendency to fault their character and rationality rather than to appreciate that considerations of the exchange process also underly their actions.

The decisions that organizations make typically require trade-offs among the total set of resources that they wish to obtain. The competitive position of the organization is determined by a balanced mix of the full range of resources. Too narrow a focus on economic resources may not produce the best overall results. For example, a prestigious image is a very valuable asset to an institution. The products that it produces are hard to measure and to evaluate in the short run, so popular perceptions of quality are particularly important. An institution that receives fewer student applicants may see its interests better served by continuing to turn away less qualified students in order to maintain its reputation as a selective campus. The economic cost of lost tuition is seen as less crucial to the institution's longer-term vitality than its academic reputation.

Because of the subtle and intangible nature of many of these non-economic resources, they are hard to identify explicitly and to weigh in decisions. Decisions that weight these resources heavily, either explicitly or implicitly, are often viewed as irrational or—pejoratively—as political. However, there can be no doubt that administrators' success often rests at least as much on how they manage these less tangible resources as on how they deal with more measurable economic variables.

Institutional researchers must be sensitive to the full range of resources when making decisions. Their failure to do so is no doubt a reason why policy makers sometimes ignore some of their analyses and recommendations. The broad view of resources may not only sensitize institutional researchers to broad considerations, of which administrators, too, may be only dimly aware, but it may also suggest some new areas for research.

Specification of Organizational Goals. A substantial amount of the scholarly literature on organizational behavior assumes that organizations are created and exist to attain goals. This conception of organizations as goal seeking is broadly accepted in much of the popular and scholarly literature on management and undoubtedly shapes the notions about management that many institutional researchers hold. However, Georgiou (1973) has suggested a counterview, which he believes better describes organizational behavior. This view conceives of an organization as composed of individuals and groups all striving to increase, maintain, or exchange the rewards (resources) that they get from the organization in return for their contributions to it. The pursuit and reconciliation of individual and group interests are the primary determinants of organizational behavior, not the pursuit of some explicit or implicit organizational goals. The decisions and courses of action taken by an organization are consequently based not on some a priori goals but on perception of the implications of complex sets of exchange relationships and mutual accommodations among affected parties, both inside and outside the organization. The various parties to these transactions all possess a variety of sources of power and seek various outcomes. Therefore, the power of top administrators (and others) is delimited by varying degrees, depending on the issues and surrounding circumstances.

Within institutions of higher education, each of the disciplines and professions has competitive as well as complementary interests. The same is true among faculty, administrators, students, and staff. The interests of governors, legislators, and state higher education agencies often conflict with those of institutions. Parents, alumni, and commercial organizations pursue conflicting as well as common objectives for an institution. The balance of power among all these and other parties shifts over time and as issues change. Under these circumstances, all the parties have some notion of what the character of the particular institution should be. What actually results, however, is a consequence of the shifting outcomes of their interactions. The interests of particular participants are served to a greater or lesser degree at various times. The institution per se does not have goals. What organizational officials seek is a balancing of multiple interests so as to provide a distribution of resources that maintains the participation of all essential members.

One should not conclude that, because organizations operate on the basis of bargaining and mutual competition among participants, they verge on anarchy and lack reasonably coherent purposes. Organizations represent an acknowledgement of the heavy weight that people place on the value of collective efforts. They are vested with strong incentives and sanctions so as to maintain members' loyalty and to assure cooperative behavior. In the contests among values and interests that take place, the values of a strong, effective organization typically rank high.

The notion of goals can limit our understanding of the complexities that shape organizational policy in another way. This problem has been addressed by Vickers (1965, p. 31), who describes policy making as "the setting of governing relations or norms, rather than in the more usual terms as the setting of goals, objectives, or ends. The difference is not merely verbal; I regard it as fundamental. I believe that great confusion results from the common assumption that all course holding can be reduced to the pursuit of an endless succession of goals."

From this perspective, organizations, such as institutions of higher education, can be viewed as made up of complex relationships among a set of variables. Changing one variable or group of variables in an organization has complex effects on other variables. Consequently, what one seeks in making decisions is a favorable set of new relationships among variables. For example, if a change in admissions policy is undertaken to improve the academic quality of incoming students but if it reduces tuition income beyond some limits, then academic quality will no longer be seen as an independent goal. A change in admissions standards could affect relationships with an important external constituentcy in negative ways; for example, the state legislature could exact retribution for such a direct but one-dimensional response to improvement of quality.

Goals are often stated in terms of one or a few variables. Little recognition is given to effects that the achievement of limited goals might have on other important variables. The notion of goals tends to obscure and oversimplify complex organizational relationships, leading to oversimplified views about courses of action and possibly risking serious unintended consequences.

Given this view of organizations, an institutional researcher is doomed to disappointment if he or she seeks clear statements of consistent, stable organizational goals. Various participants state their interests in ways that enhance their bargaining positions and maintain their flexibility to accommodate new intelligence on the positions and power relationships of various parties. Even when there is a consensus among participants, the shape of desired future relationships is so complex that they rarely can be specified in simple goal statements intended to guide specific actions. Goals generally have to be stated broadly to accommodate a variety of interests and to avoid a misleading appearance of precision.

View of Organizational Issues as Solvable Problems. Unsatisfactory situations in institutions are often referred to as problems. An organizational problem is often viewed as analogous to a mathematical problem. It is assumed that the problem has one best solution and that, once it has been solved, it should no longer present difficulties. Those possessing the solution can then proceed with confidence to apply it to other relevant situations. This problem-solving perspective on organizational conditions may misrepresent the actual nature of institutions and the character of policy- and decision-making processes.

The open systems view of organizations, which holds that organizations are composed of many parties who interact to pursue their own interests and who have to reconcile those self-interests with the organization's collective interests, suggests that a large class of decisions deals with the reconciliation of conflicting values. The substantive and procedural ends sought by various parties differ, and these differences must be resolved sufficiently if the collective enterprise is to function. The resolution of value conflicts represented by particular decisions, however, generally does not alter the underlying basic interests of the parties. They only temporarily subordinate some interests in order to preserve other, perhaps more important, interests. The basic interests remain and tend to reemerge periodically as new opportunities arise to reopen discussion. From this perspective, conflicts or "problems" remain; they are not solved in a permanent sense. They lie more or less submerged awaiting a favorable opportunity to resurface. Over time, organizational attention shifts from one to another of these value conflict issues as changing conditions or perspectives prioritize various concerns. Cohen and others (1972) suggest that many such organizational issues arise in an almost accidental or random way to command attention.

One implication of this perspective—that "problems" are never solved but only temporarily accommodated—is that there are few if any general prescriptions for organizational issues that can be applied across a wide variety of settings. There are some common approaches to conflict clarification and resolution, and there are some general agreements on fundamental values, but the actual solutions to the specific conflicts in a particular setting depend on complex interactions among the participants, who all seek their own best interest. The participants' interests, of course, include preserving the collective benefits provided by the organization, not just their immediate personal rewards.

The slowness and the politics that attend the making of decisions in institutions of higher education are apt to be frustrating to an institutional researcher who views problems as primarily technical questions that are solvable and nonrecurring once solved. An understanding that organizational decision making is not problem solving in the mathematical or technical sense may not make life easier, but it will perhaps make life more understandable and possibly less frustrating. Certainly, it should help institutional researchers to perceive the nature and role of their contributions in the complex world of institutional governance and management more clearly.

Organizational Location of Institutional Research. Institutional research offices are located in a variety of places in campus organization structures. Many report to the chief academic officer. Frequently they report to a vice-president for planning or for planning and budget. Some report to the president's staff assistants. Others report to the chief business officer, director of administrative computing, or some other administrative staff officer. At some campuses, units at two or more locations engage in institutional research-type activities.

Political theories of organizational structure suggest that the organizational location of the institutional research function has significant implications for its influence on policy and decisions. Redford (1969, pp. 29–30) sets forth this notion as follows: "Decisions on administrative organization reflect the expectation that certain kinds of interests will be promoted by the kind of organization chosen. The weight of forums accrues from the interests they represent and from the strategic position they occupy in decision-making processes." This view of organizational structure suggests that the location of an institutional research office has some important consequences. Such offices are sources of power for those who have access to them. Presumably, those to whom an institutional research office reports have prime access to its services. Also, the power of the institutional research office is likely to be affected by constraints surrounding its location. The interest of the supervising office is likely to take precedence over the interests of more remote offices.

The influence on an institutional research office rests primarily on the value that clients place on the data analyses and advice that it provides. Various administrators place a different value on the utility of data and analyses in decision mkaing. Nevertheless, there is a general expectation among many of those in institutions, and certainly among those in external agencies concerned with higher education, that important decisions should be based, to the extent possible, on data and analysis. Therefore, the ability to obtain accurate, credible, and consistent data and insightful analyses gives an official an important source of influence.

The reciprocal relationship between the host office and institutional research also holds true: The influence and priorities of institutional research are affected by the influence and interests of its host. If the office to which the institutional research unit reports lacks influence, then the possibility that institutional research will have an influence is lessened. Some implications that various locations hold for institutional research offices are described in the paragraphs that follow.

When institutional research is attached to a unit low in the hierarchy, it tends to be isolated from environmental information and from central policy concerns. Its guidance on policy issues is filtered through intervening layers. Its data and studies are likely to be evaluated in the context of perceptions of the character and motivations of intervening offices. Isolation from top echelons also lessens the influence of institutional research on data quality issues and on its ability to get the cooperation needed for conducting studies. Under such circumstances, institutional research is apt to be less aware of the political implication of issues.

Campus planning and budgeting offices are primary clients of institutional research. The close relationships among these functions suggest that they should be closely associated. Often this does not occur. Academics are apt to view the power represented by the managerial functions of planning, budget, evaluation, and institutional research as giving emphasis to bureaucratic rather than to professional values. People's view of this situation is apt to be colored by whether they believe that institutions are overbureaucratized and overadministered or that they are inefficient, ineffective, or both because they are underadministered.

Institutional research is often located in the office of a vice-president. Such a location tends to emphasize the interests of the host office. However, the host has to wear two hats. It must both attend to its own data and research needs and to those of other campus units. The host's priorities are apt to receive first consideration even if an institutionwide perspective might not rank them as high. Location is a subordinate unit may result in reluctance to have institutional research "meddle" in the activities of peer or superordinate units and for those units to be tempted to resist intrusion into their affairs.

Location within the president's office overcomes the parochialism resulting from location within subordinate offices as well as potential conflicts of interest. Priorities are more apt to reflect an institutionwide perspective. Institutional research is likely also to have readier access to information on external trends and campuswide issues. The influence of the institutional research office is associated with campuswide priorities rather than with the possibly more partisan perspectives of a subordinate unit.

The institutional research function can also be located in two or more campus units, which serves to decentralize its activities. Various campus units could thus set their own research priorities and avoid the dilemmas that a single institutional office confronts when having to decide among a host of competing priorities. Nearly every office on a campus needs data on its own operations and on external trends affecting its operations. Central research offices can be insensitive to the data needs of subordinate units. In any case, they rarely have sufficient resources to address the full range of needs of the various units on campus. Thus, to some extent, institutional research must take place in nearly all units. However, recognition of the data and research requirements of individual units should not detract from the important roles of a central campus office. Too great a dispersion of institutional research can lead to duplication of effort, failure to give concerted attention to campuswide priorities, and potentially disruptive competition among individual units. The possibility of having two or more differing sets of "official" numbers on a given topic increases. Decentralization also loses some advantages of scale, and computer center staff could be caught between inconsistently defined requests for the same kinds of data. The advent of microcomputers, as noted earlier, will facilitate the decentralization of institutional research, but it raises many problems that are discussed elsewhere in this volume.

Of course, many other considerations are involved in the location of the institutional research function. Often, the placement of an institutional research office hinges in the capabilities and interests of particular campus officials. The individual most sensitive to technical concerns surrounding planning and budgeting may be assigned the function because that person most values its contribution or because the president believes that person is best suited to supervise and use its services. Nevertheless, one should be sensitive to the political implications of location that have just been described.

Conclusions

The circumstances that higher education now confronts are changing the demands of governance and management processes. These changing governance and management demands are likely to shape the focus of institutional research. Among the factors affecting it are the many facets of retrenchment, the growth of financial aid, and continuing concern for quality. New technologies are increasing the capabilities of institutional research, but they are also posing problems of coordination and consistency as data-processing and analytic capacity become more diffused throughout institutions. At the same time, new conceptions of organizational behavior are requiring institutional researchers to rethink the role they play in institutions and how they can better serve the kinds of policy and decision processes described by these emerging theories. They must be sensitive to the role that data and analysis plays in policy and decision making, the contexts in which they are used, the multiple criteria that must be balanced in assessments of organizational effectiveness, and the weaknesses in traditional concepts of goals and problems. The location of institutional research in institutions must be assessed for its political implications. The demand for institutional research is likely to keep it vigorous. However, the function may be threatened during severe budget reductions if its contributions are not viewed as relevant to central campus concerns.

References

Blau, P. M. *Exchange and Power in Social Life.* New York: Wiley, 1964.
Breneman, D. "Economic Trends: What Do They Imply for Higher Education?" *AAHE Bulletin,* 1979, *32* (1), 1-5.
Cohen, M. D., March, J. G., and Olsen, J. P. "A Garbage Can Model of Organizational Choice." *Administrative Science Quarterly,* 1972, *17* (1), 1-25.
Georgiou, P. "The Goal Paradigm and Notes Toward a Counter Paradigm." *Administrative Science Quarterly,* 1973, *18* (3), 291-31.
Gerth, H. H., and Mills, C. W. *From Max Weber: Essays in Sociology.* New York: Oxford University Press, 1946.
Glenny, L. A. "Demographic and Related Issues for Higher Education in the 1980s." *Journal of Higher Education,* 1980, *51,* 303-350.
Glenny, L. A., and Schmidtlein, F. A. "The Role of the State in the Governance of Higher Education." *Educational Evaluation and Policy Analysis,* 1983, *5* (2), 133-153.
Homans, G. *Social Behavior: Its Elementary Forms.* New York: Harcourt Brace Jovanovich, 1961.
Hyatt, J. A., Schulman, C. H., and Santiago, A. A. *Reallocation: Strategies for Effective Resource Management.* Washington, D.C.: National Association of College and University Business Officers, 1984.
Ilchman, W. F., and Uphoff, N. T. *The Political Economy of Change.* Berkeley: University of California Press, 1971.
Katz, D., and Kahn, R. L. *The Social Psychology of Organizations.* New York: Wiley, 1966.
Keller, G. *Academic Strategy: The Management Revolution in American Higher Education.* Baltimore, Md.: Johns Hopkins University Press, 1983.

Kerr, C. *Presidents Make a Difference: Strengthening Leadership in Colleges and Universities.* Washington, D.C.: Association of Governing Boards of Universities and Colleges, 1984.

Kuhn, T. S. *The Structure of Scientific Revolutions.* Chicago: University of Chicago Press, 1962.

Mingle, J. R., and Associates. *Challenges of Retrenchment: Strategies for Consolidating Programs, Cutting Costs, and Reallocating Resources.* San Francisco: Jossey-Bass, 1981.

Peters, T. J., and Waterman, R. H., Jr. *In Search of Excellence.* New York: Harper & Row, 1982.

Redford, E. S. *Democracy in the Administrative State.* New York: Oxford University Press, 1969.

Shirley, R. C. "Limiting the Scope of Strategy: A Decision-Based Approach." *Academy of Management Review,* 1982, 7 (2), 262–268.

Study Group on the Conditions of Excellence in American Higher Education. *Involvement in Learning: Realizing the Potential of American Higher Education.* Washington, D.C.: National Institute of Education, 1984.

Tetlow, W. L. (Ed). *Using Microcomputers for Planning and Management Support.* New Directions for Institutional Research, no. 44. San Francisco: Jossey-Bass, 1984.

Vickers, G. *The Art of Judgment.* New York: Basic Books, 1965.

Frank Schmidtlein is assistant professor of higher education in the Department of Educational Policy, Planning, and Administration at the University of Maryland, College Park. From 1980 to 1984 he served as assistant to the chancellor; the Office of Institutional Studies reported to him during that period.

Decision support technology presents institutional researchers with opportunities to build on their experiences with institutional decision making and hence to provide new decision support services that no other professionals can supply.

Telematics and the Decision Support Intermediary

Bernard S. Sheehan

This chapter reviews developments in information technology that are said to be reshaping analytical and management decision practices in higher education. It addresses the question, How will these developments change the analytical role of decision making and institutional processes for doing and using the analysis produced by institutional research?

The chapter focuses on how advanced communication and computing technologies affect institutional research–related roles. As these decision-making and decision support roles come under the influence of changing technology, there are implications for the organization and content of institutional research as well. The turbulence caused by rapid change in technology limits the following comments to the short term. One important conclusion is that practitioners will increasingly study ways in which decision support, the traditional purpose of institutional research, can make the most of the information-rich environment of the late 1980s.

In order to examine the impacts of changing information technology, it is necessary to describe institutional research precisely. Yet, over the twenty-

The author thanks a number of colleagues for their help in the preparation of this chapter. In particular he is grateful for insights and critiques from Kenneth Brown, Stephen Hample, Paul Jedamus, Peter Newsted, and Mike Stevenson.

five years since the first forum on institutional research was held, there has not been agreement on an explicit definition. Practitioners and theoreticians from different regions of the world and from different types of postsecondary institutions have not agreed, and the field, as seen from all these perspectives, has evolved over time. But, if institutional research is undefined or not definable, how can change be measured, noticed, or even discussed? What would be the parameters or dimensions of change? Thus, the logical basis of the speculation in this chapter depends, in the first instance, on how we choose to describe institutional research.

Dimensions of Change

The functional definition presented later in this chapter provides the first dimension of change to be examined as a result of changing information technology. This definition permits discussion of change in activities, tasks, functions, and processes as well as of change in the required skills, background, and disciplinary perspectives of professionals working in institutional research. The second dimension is organizational in the sense that it affects how these elemental activities are structured into units within the institution, and therefore it is concerned with the personnel, operations, planning, control, and marketing aspects of human organizations. The remaining two dimensions are content and context. Context is concerned with the larger structural or organizational questions related to the institution and to postsecondary education in the political and economic jurisdiction or region. The dimension of content is like the other dimensions, intuitively clear but quickly becoming awkward when we attempt to set up measures. I suggest that the uses of the analyses produced by institutional research are proxy for content.

Measurement and experimental questions aside, analysis of impacts on organizations is a challenging concept. It is difficult to separate causes and effects from a tangle of scientific, legal, political, economic, and psychological aspects, even in retrospect (Pool, 1977). Nonetheless, there are certain relationships that can provide a starting point. The following framework does not remove the complexities involved in trying to understand how some scientific breakthrough, say in the physics underlying microelectronics, will change a human organization like a university, but it does suggest some of the questions that we need to address.

Six elements, thought of as an impact analysis framework, are technology, applications, impact sectors, planning and analysis, future, and change (Sheehan, 1982). Technologies give rise to applications in teaching, research, and administration that affect organizational units and people, that is, the impact sectors of the institution. Planning and analysis processes are themselves affected, which, together with the scope of the impacts on society in general, suggest that futures research could provide insight into how institutional planning might evolve (Morrison and others, 1983). The lessons learned from decades of resistance to innovation in higher education provide a basis for anticipating institutional responses to change (Friedman, 1982).

While the analysis in this chapter cannot address the full range of issues suggested by this impact analysis framework, it will be guided by the six elements. Similarly, all important consequences to the dimensions of change are not developed here, although repeated mention of them helps to emphasize the extent to which technology has already permeated higher education and hence how hard it is to separate cause from effect.

What Is Changing

Before we zero in on the main focus of the chapter and study the implications of changing information applications for the decision and analysis activities that comprise institutional research-related roles, it is useful to set out what, at least in the short term, we can say is changing and what is not.

Moore's Law. Following the impact analysis framework, we look first at the underlying technology. There are some important and unusual features about microelectronic engineering and the physics underlying chip making that are important for our estimation of the scope of the impacts. The number of electronic components in an integrated circuit has been doubling every year for nearly a quarter of a century. Chip technology is still far from the fundamental limits imposed by physics, and it seems reasonable to assume that this phenomenon, known as Moore's law (Martin, 1981), will be more or less sustained at least through this decade. The significance of packing more and more components onto a chip is that the resulting devices are faster, cheaper, and smaller and that they have increased memory. Surprisingly, all the desirable features improve, and all the undesirable characteristics are mitigated. Advances are more rapid and profound than we have witnessed with other technologies, which generally require that engineers make difficult trade-off choices between good and bad properties.

The fact that Moore's law not only models the past of microprocessors but seems to be a creditable indicator of the future of the underlying engineering gives us confidence that these remarkable rates will continue. Moreover, advances in the underlying science take time to work their way through the microelectronic technologies and markets, and these advances in electronic components take even longer to have an impact on the devices used in higher education. Thus, we can be confident that, to the extent that improvement in these device technologies leads to improvement in such applications as personal computers, word processors, and electronic mail, the cascade of change will certainly continue into the next decade.

This is an important conclusion. We do not have a situation characterized by technological advance followed by a period of organizational adaptation. We have instead a situation characterized by past and current rapid advance and accelerated future advances. This is a more complex problem of impact analysis. The accelerating technologies are spawning many overlapping applications, each potentially having its unique consequence for the impact sectors and for planning and analysis processes themselves and each posing its own assimilation challenge to the institution.

The Stages Hypothesis. Common sense (and institutional research experience with enrollment projections) says that all trends must eventually moderate and subside. Nolan's (1982) stage hypothesis is often used in the study of organizational assimilation or learning about a technology (Cash and others, 1983). Essentially, it says that technologies pass through four stages as they are successfully implemented in an organization: technology identification and investment, technology learning and adoption, rationalization and management control, and maturity or widespread technology transfer.

The problems of managing the functional, organizational, contextual, and content changes produced as a technology climbs through Nolan's S curve are still present. However, the predictablity of change suggested by the stage hypothesis is a welcomed analytical and management tool. Also, the recognition that one manages and responds to technologies differently as they pass through each stage yields some clues when we attempt to anticipate impacts.

The important conclusion that follows from Moore's law and from the stage hypothesis is that institutions of higher education will have to deal, at least for the next ten years, with a bewildering array of rapidly changing technologies all at different phases of their implementation by the higher education community and by individual institutions. However, while the resultant management of impacts is still enormously complex, it is made more tractable by the stages insight. We can anticipate something of the tangled growth and assimilation patterns of technologies and hence the challenges and opportunities that intelligent devices present to institutional planning and management.

Telematics. Although institutional researchers did not use the term *information technology* extensively a decade ago, it has become central to much of the literature. The perception of information technology as computer hardware or software is common, yet it tends to mask information technology as communications. It is, after all, communications that are the significant management use made of information technology, not computing (Gerola and Gomory, 1984). Text processing, communications, file transfer, electronic bulletin boards, electronic mail, and conferencing have turned the computer into a general-purpose technology for the distribution of information on campus and between institutions. The rapid convergence of telecommunications, computerized data processing, and office automation into a unitary technology and, more important, into a single cluster of concepts about the means by which information-related tasks are accomplished, is important enough to risk the use of the term *telematics*. Telematics as *converging* computing and communications systems appropriately describes the dynamic nature of this technology, which is seen as one of the fundamental change agents in an age of change—indeed, an information age.

Software. Software developments, although not yet as conspicuous as hardware advances, are beginning to accelerate. Important to institutional research are the popular end user packages, which include data base management systems, graphics, word processing facilities, and spreadsheet capabilities. Automation of institutional research spreadsheet analysis has taken a good deal of the tedium out of many standard calculations and moved practical computer-based modeling studies considerably ahead (Brown and Droegemueller, 1983). The next advances are the fourth-generation languages, the nonprocedural systems like FOCUS, RAMIS, MAPPER, and NPL, many of which are becoming increasingly accessible on micros. These languages free institutional researchers from having to write computer procedural codes and permit them to retain control over the development and maintenance of computer-based systems essential to the effective operation of the institutional research office (Sholtys, 1983).

There are other advances that seem sure to make the work environment of the decision maker quite different in the longer term from our current experience (Huber, 1984). These applications include the artificial intelligence–based knowledge systems or expert systems, which have already found significant use as decision support systems in an increasing number of professional applications (Hayes-Roth and others, 1983). These systems amass much of the knowledge in a narrow specialty field and make it available to practitioners in that field in a convenient, timely, and practical way. Knowledge systems have the ability to learn from their own experience and from that of the experts who assisted in their initial programming. For the purposes of the analysis here, I assume the practical impact of expert systems and of intelligent robots on our institutional research context is beyond the short-term limit of this chapter.

Some Persistent Features

It is easy to overlook the fact that, while we are in the midst of a technological revolution, some things are not changing or are changing so slowly as not to seem changed within the increasingly short time frames that are important. Among the sorts of constants that are relevant to our functional, organizational, content, and context dimensions of change are decision determinants like institutional culture, the fundamentals of data processing, and the ways in which institutions make decisions.

Institutional Culture. The essential values and traditions of individual institutions remain mostly constant. These traits of institutional culture include traditions of faculty dominance or administration dominance, excellence in undergraduate teaching, excellence in certain disciplines, dedication to community service, and so on. Thus, it seems reasonable to assume, for example, that in the immediate future the job of institutional research will be set by the personality of a strong campus leader no more and no less than it has in the immediate past.

Basics of Data Processing. What we understand as the essence of data processing does not change significantly in the short time periods that we sometimes characterize as the "generations" of information technologies. Both the constancy of the basics of data processing in the face of technological change and the consequences for institutional research can be illustrated as follows: Personal computers are complex systems. The hardware is advancing rapidly even in its architecture and component configurations. Operating systems are evolving to keep up with the need to match the new hardware with the even more volatile software packages.

This ebb and flow is not new to data processing; it is the standard work environment for computer centers. However, the institutional researcher who has become dependent on personal or end user technologies is hard-pressed to give the important systems decisions the priority that they require. The following six points illustrate that the complexity of information systems persists even though computers are slickly packaged as user-friendly consumer items and sold in department stores:

1. Hardware: How and when should you upgrade your basic components?

2. Memory: When and at what cost should the elements of your memory be expanded?

3. Printers: What characteristics and features should your system have? What are enhancements worth to you?

4. Communications: Which networks should you join? What investment in time should you make studying the various mainframes to which you could be connected? What modem characteristics do you acquire and at what cost?

5. Operation Systems: If you think of the operating system as the means that matches the hardware with various other software, such as compilers (languages) and packages (word processors, spreadsheets, nonprocedural languages, communications facilities, graphics), you see the myriad of decisions about operating systems that are technical as well as economic. The decisions related to operating systems are often not framed in the functional language of institutional research but in the technical language of data processing.

6. End User Software: A bewildering array of software packages is available. The choice of what package, what version, when to acquire, and at what cost are all important and difficult decisions. One's options here depend on the other systems options, and they are limited by turmoil in the software industry.

These six points serve to indicate that the institutional researcher may not be able to avoid many of the traditional computer center problems that challenge data processing (DP) professionals. In other words, the power and elegance of new information technology not only offers the promise of potent support, but it comes bundled with many generic DP challenges. These challenges are insidious, because the institutional researcher is not prepared for them, is not forewarned of them by the vendors, and may not place them in the proper perspective as generic data processing problems.

Institutional Decision-Related Processes. Another invariant is the dependency of management and decision processes on human intervention. Although few expect to see in this decade unaided robots making university planning and management decisions, there seems to be the perception that technology will simplify decision processes by automating some of the steps or procedures. This conclusion may arise because of a misconception of the role of information in decision support and the inherent complexity of real-world problems (Mason and Mitroff, 1981). Consider the institutional planning process to illustrate the point that individual steps in the decision process can be greatly assisted and improved and that the entire process can be enhanced without changing the process itself.

There are many ways of characterizing the process of developing and implementing a plan at the institutional level. For our purposes, let us agree that the process can be modeled by general steps, such as the following: formulation of general goals, statement of objectives for a period, planning of programs to meet objectives, implementation of programmatic decisions, report on and evaluation of activities and outcomes, and review of objectives and programs. Two additional considerations are who is involved in each step and what these people provide to the process at each step. In many cases, the participants supply information, but other inputs include assumptions, reviews, proposals, recommendations, assessments, commitments, judgments, measurements, and decisions. We appeal to the steps of the familiar planning process and to the role of information as input to circumscribe the relatively modest impact of information on the intrinsic complexity of planning as a process that is fundamentally structural. Telematics, including expert systems, is likely to change planning processes in the 1990s by making processes that better model the complexity of real-world decision problems humanly possible.

This is not to deny that information technology will have significant short-term impacts on planning in higher education. Personal computers permit decision makers to be better informed and equipped to use information from a wide variety of sources, to communicate, and to test their own theories. However, the framework for this enhanced use of better information is still the planning process as determined by institutional culture. Thus, the near-term bound is set on the influence of personal computers. None of the essential steps can be removed simply by the application of information technology, even though institutions can improve planning processes. Enhanced planning results are achieved primarily by improvements in the efficiency and effectiveness of human processes and inputs, not by removing essential steps.

Elements That May Be Changing

In the absence of longitudinal data from the field, it is necessary to speculate on certain other elements of our functional, organizational, content, and context change dimensions. We will return to the question of data gathering later.

Structures. The literature of institutional research has dealt with, over a number of years, questions of how an office ought to be organized, to whom the director ought to report, and various other questions about the internal sturcture of the office and its external relations. However, there is no experimental evidence that plots changes in organizational structure over the last two decades. Anecdotally and intuitively, most of us know of, or at least anticipate, structural change in institutional research as a result of information technology. But, without more evidence it seems an item that we ought to leave as "may be changing" for the present.

The Greening of Institutional Research. While we have done many studies on the aging professoriate and its consequences for postsecondary education, there are no corresponding data for those engaged in institutional research. Yet it seems reasonable to assume that the number of years of experience for the average practitioner is increasing and that it has been increasing for at least a decade. The extent to which such variables would have a direct impact on the function, organization, content, and context questions is at the least an interesting speculation. In the longer term, increased use of expert systems may well free practitioners from a concentration on quantitative methodologies and permit them to balance their study of the phenomena of higher education with increased use of qualitative methods (Kuhns and Martorana, 1982), including those that are sensitive to basic human values.

Telematics as an Institutional Research Specialty. The widespread introduction of computer and communications applications across campuses has caused a centralization-decentralization flux (King, 1983), which has created a need for decision support on telematics questions themselves. This, and the challenges persisting from the unchanging basics of data processing discussed earlier, may yield markets for institutional research services. However, the extent of dislocation created by the evolution of data processing from a central service to a distributed utility has not yet been widely studied (McCredie, 1983); hence, its consequences are speculative. Also, it may be wise to consider that, while most writers agree that the computing environment five years hence will be quite different from today's, there are many things that will not change much in the short term. For campus administrative services units, this list includes the existing portfolio of major applications, the multiyear backlog of new applications development, the shortage of skilled people, and the continuing growth in central DP capacity (Canning, 1984).

Functions of Institutional Research in Transition

The purpose of this section is to set out in as much detail as practical a functional description of institutional research that most practitioners can accept as a starting point. The description must build on the fundamental tasks or human processes associated with institutional research so that it provides a suitable basis for analysis of impacts. The framework depicted in

Figure 1 assumes that decision support is the essential rationale for institutional research and associates three central roles with it. These roles are those of decision maker, decision support intermediary, and technologist who is expert in information, computing, and communications technologies.

The activities or steps necessary to accomplish these three roles help to describe institutional research. These activities and the relationships among them are the targets of possible change agents. The merit of the framework approach is that it makes as explicit as possible the assumptions, variables, and functional parameters that are the focus of current considerations. Like any model, the framework abstraction is not as rich as reality, but it does provide bases for criticism of the conclusions drawn here and for evaluation of more useful models or constructs. For purposes of the current speculation, the framework is taken to represent a commonsense understanding of institutional research. The dashed lines in Figure 1 indicate communication between the roles, while solid lines indicate articulation among the individual functions or steps characterized by the boxes.

Decision Maker Role. This role is modeled essentially as that of problem solver. Of course, there is no one way in which all decision makers think (Isenberg, 1984), but the model proposed attempts to span a range of alternatives. As shown in the framework, the role is consistent with both the "rational/comprehensive" and the "incremental/remedial" paradigms of decision making

Figure 1. Institutional Research-Related Roles

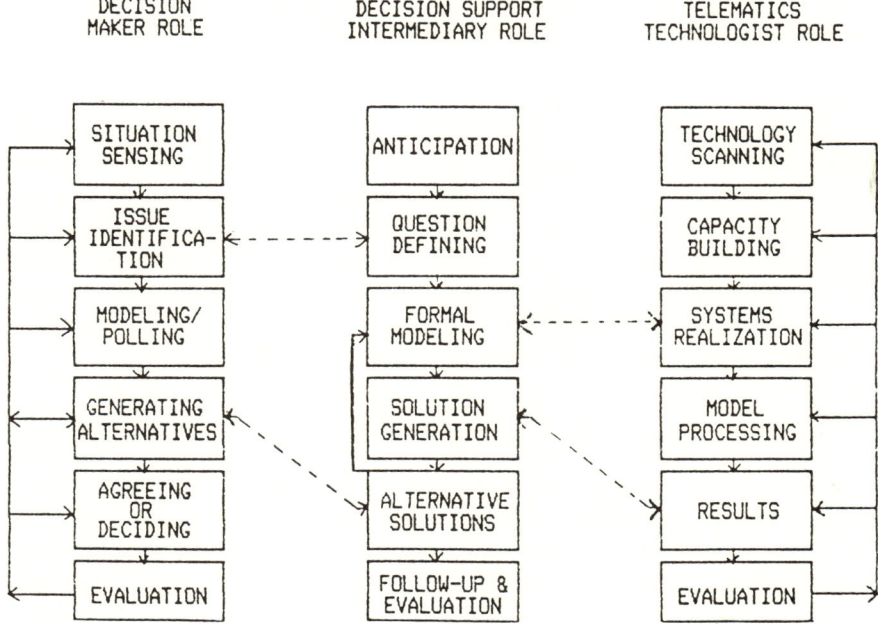

(Schmidtlein, 1974). Thus, the role of the decision maker is seen as involving a person who is sensitive to situations surrounding the decision context and who proceeds by identifying certain issues. The way the process continues depends on the decision style of the incumbent, who seeks to generate alternatives either by attempting to form a consensus among the opinions of advisers and important players or by some more formal, rational modeling process. Once the alternatives have been generated and the important players agree or some more objective decision criteria has been applied, the decision maker moves on to implement or manage the decision and prepares to receive feedback that will help to evaluate the decision and the process followed to reach it.

Telematics Technologist Role. The technologist more or less constantly monitors or scans technological developments that may affect the ability of the institutional research unit to specify the computer-based systems that may have to be realized or constructed. The role of the technologist further involves the actual processing or running of models, including data input, so as to produce computer-based results that will be useful in the institutional research response. This role also involves evelution of the results produced over time and hence continual evaluation of the processes that lead to the results.

Decision Support Intermediary Role. Most people associate the decision support intermediary role with the professional institutional researcher. This role involves anticipating not only the general category of questions that the office will be asked to address but also the resources that will be necessary to provide the decision maker with meaningful alternative solutions. In any particular instance, however, the role will involve the clear definition of questions put to the office and a problem-solving sequence of steps that most often tends to be rational rather than incremental and that leads to the generation of presentable alternative solutions. The professional responsibilities of the decision support intermediary are such that the alternative solutions may require follow-up that is beyond the particular matter being dealt with; of course, the intermediary also has ongoing responsibility for evaluation of the solutions actually presented and of all processes involved in arriving at them.

Interaction Between Roles. The framework is as lean as possible so that we can focus on essentials. The modeled circumstance has the decision maker discussing a particular identified issue with the intermediary. The two-way dialogue leads the intermediary to establish a clear definition of the question that must be researched. Once solutions are available, the dialogue is reopened, and the institutional research alternatives become part of the decision maker's process of generating choices for consideration. The discussion of alternatives often takes into account some of the more subjective questions and issues that the more formal or objective institutional research determination of alternatives has not emphasized. The process of dialogue may not end here; for example, it can lead to insights that cause the process to cycle back through issue identification and question definition until the decision maker is satisfied.

For current purposes, the interface between the intermediary and the technologist is as shown in Figure 1. Once the intermediary has a reasonably firm fix on the important variables and their relationships, a discussion can be held with the technologist on how to build a computer-based system that will produce the results of information needed. Once the model results are available, the technologist and the intermediary discuss them, and, as in the previous case, the process may be repeated until the intermediary is satisfied that the alternative solutions address the question defined and present a suitable spectrum of alternatives for the particular decision maker under the present circumstances.

It is time to emphasize that Figure 1 describes a set of interrelated roles that are abstractions or models. When a person performs one of the processes entailed in a given role, then that person is playing that role, regardless of his or her organizational position, title, or institutional responsibilities. A single person may play all three roles, and any role may be played by more than one person. Often, the decision maker is a committee, and the intermediary is a team of analysts.

Analysis of Impacts. With the framework in place, we are now in a position to use it to gain insight into how new technology affects the processes or steps associated with these decision-related roles and hence into how it affects institutional research. On the basis of the argument that in the short term decision processes depend more on institutional culture than on changing information technology, we conclude that the twelve human tasks that model the roles of the decision maker and the decision support intermediary are not as directly affected as the tasks associated with the telematics technologist.

Each of the six functions that make up the role of the telematics technologist is sensitive to changing information technology. The rate of change of technology and the state of the art at any given time are both the outcome sought from technology scans and an important determinant of the complexity of the task itself. These factors determine the human resources that ought to be expended on the scanning activity and the physical and financial resources necessary to support investigations of existing and developing technology that may have significance for institutional research. The task of technology scanning is becoming a continuing activity. Individuals who are already technically competent and aware of the current state of the art require time each day not only to read the literature but also to experiment with new hardware and software so as to appreciate practical decision support strengths and limitations.

The simplest way of thinking of the activity of capacity building is as the link between an appreciation of available technology and the actual building or realization of a particular system or facility. As data processing equipment and services have changed over the past two decades, the task of managing capacity-building activities has become much more complex. If one is providing in batch mode a finite set of standard services, capacity building is relatively straightforward. However, the dominance is now shifting from the information systems department to the end user, who wants systems that are completely and immediately responsive to the user's changing requirements (Huff and Rivard, 1983). It is quite a different task to provide a capacity that is essentially a decision support system generator than it is to provide only a portfolio of standard data processing services.

The systems realization function involves the technologist in a dialogue with the intermediary for the purpose of determining system specifications. Once the two have agreed what the system ought to do, the technologist's role is to build the system. Again, the task is sensitive to changing technology and to expectations about information technology created by the media and by end user experience with personal computers and other new technologies. For example, institutional researchers have studied for many years the most appropriate way of presenting alternative solutions to busy decision makers. Practitioners learned early that not only the content of the results of institutional research was important but that all aspects of its presentation could be critical to its effectiveness (Hackman, 1983). Today, the decision about how solutions can best be presented to the decision maker involves considerations of alternative communications technology. Sometimes, solutions should go over the electronic mail system or through other elements of the office automation system. For some decision makers, it is best simply to pass them a floppy disk.

Model processing is the actual manipulation of the system to achieve results, including input of data and the usual technical verification that results are what they appear to be. Except as implied by the previous discussion, technology change has not yet affected this activity in significant ways beyond the fact that the systems being manipulated are much more flexible and powerful. The final activity of evaluation can be thought of as an introductory phase of technology scan. That is, the experience in building the capacity and actual system, running it, and assessing the validity and usefulness of the results leads to an evaluation of the process that helps to provide criteria for the more or less unstructured tasks associated with most aspects of technology scanning.

As we study the effects of changing information technology on the functions of the telematics technologist role, we begin to appreciate how changing technology indirectly affects the functions of the other roles. As part of the decision support intermediary's charge of anticipating future developments, he or she must think ahead to gauge the total resources needed to provide the institutional research service. That process will be informed by the technologist's technology-scanning activities. It is obvious that the formal modeling activities are influenced by discussions with the telematics technologist about the specifications required for the computer-based activities leading to retrieval of information from computer data bases or resulting from simulations or other model manipulation activities. In the same way, the presentation of alternative results as input to the decision maker's activity of generating alternatives depends on the media used.

Organization of Institutional Research

In the preceding section, we concluded that the activities of the telematics technologist are profoundly affected by, indeed inextricably tied to, changes in information technology. It therefore seems sensible to examine the organizational implications. Because of the traditional relationship between institutional research and data processing (Staman, 1979), as the telematics technologist role itself demonstrates, there are some difficult organizational issues facing not only institutional research and information systems departments but whole institutions as they attempt to respond to pent-up end user demand for information services.

The increased visibility and significance of the telematics technologist role suggests that three questions about organization will have to be asked. First, should the telematics technologist role be an office of institutional research responsibility? As currently constituted, offices of institutional research seem to cover the whole spectrum, ranging from very little to significant information technology activities. Second, if the telematics technologist role is not to be a responsibility of institutional research, then what ought to be the organizational arrangements through which the office of institutional research acquires access to the services of a telematics technologist? Related questions bear on how the institution will respond organizationally to end user demands from both academics and administrators. Third, if the office of institutional research embraces the essence of the telematics technologist role organizationally (as it must functionally), does this present challenges or opportunities? There are little data on current practice and trends.

With respect to other types of organizations, the literature on the notion of the information center (IC) is growing. The notion originated with I.B.M. Canada in 1974. ICs make tools, advice, and training available to those who wish to do their own computing. The IC concept has evolved to take in personal computing (Guimaraes, 1984) and office automation. In some organizations, the IC is seen as the most effective way of addressing end user needs. Since ICs share many features with the academic computer services center, it seems reasonable to expect that IC-type units will flourish on college and university campuses.

An important organizational question follows from the decision to make the telematics technologist role a responsibility of the institutional research office: Is institutional research to provide IC-type services to end users, as some authors suggest (Stevenson and Walleri, 1983, 1984; Paschke and others, 1984; Sheehan, 1984)? The concern expressed by Jedamus (Hample, 1983) that "information anarchy" could follow if numerous campus decision centers exploit telematics has led to recognition of the need for coordinated and integrated decision support (Norris and Mims, 1984) and to the suggestion that institutional research can assume a decision support management (DSM) function as a natural evolution of current practice (Jedamus,

1984). It may be that the path to institutional research predominance in DSM will include an apprenticeship as an IC.

Incorporation of IC services into the office of institutional research will raise a number of management questions, including the compatibility of the new functions, staffing, the implications for the office of adding new types of clients, the skill sets required, and the compatibility of the somewhat different perspectives needed. It is difficult to deal with these questions in general, but it seems clear that the critical factors for success by institutional research in these areas include continued anticipation as well as increased adaptability. The question comes down in the end to one of providing valuable services, perhaps even unique services, for which there is no other source. Each institutional research unit must examine its own portfolio of services and assess the risk factors so as to determine how the current and planned job mix can be adjusted to minimize organizational risk.

Context and Content of Institutional Research

Changing information technology is one of the topics most discussed on many campuses as institutions grapple with issues ranging from the acquisition of supercomputers to the provision of ever more sophisticated computer-assisted learning systems, all in an environment that is increasingly characterized by personal computers on professors' desks and in students' homes and by networks tying them all together. Hence, this chapter will not address many of the content and context questions about the impact of changing information technology, because they are not peculiar to institutional research. Clearly, institutional research must provide information to support telematic decisions, whether they be in planning, resource allocation, evaluation, or other areas of management. However, as a direct change agent these content effects seem similar to the evolutionary processes that institutional researchers have gone through in the past as they have learned to provide the information needed to support decisions in whatever the area of concern or crisis was at the time.

This notwithstanding, and recalling the organizational implications of the changes in the telematics technologist role discussed earlier, institutional research units seem to have an opportunity to fill the vacuum on many campuses for information centers. Such units should develop and enhance their skill sets and experience in many aspects of the new information technology. This will strengthen the capacity of the decision support intermediary to provide information that can support decisions related to telematics itself.

What is true of individual campuses is also true of the society at large. Ours is increasingly an information society. While this does not pinpoint the particular requirements for institutional research, it does imply that institutional researchers, like other professionals, need an increased awareness, sensitivity, and literacy with respect to the consequences of the information revolution. In the longer term, content changes will be imputed to changes in the ways in which data, the results of analysis, information, knowledge, insight from human experience, and advice are used in institutional processes related to evalution, management, allocation, and planning.

Research Possibilities

Researchers who wish to study the impact of technology on aspects of institutional research are hampered by a lack of experimental data. This is not a unique circumstance, in part because it is difficult to determine the important parameters and measures and to devise experiments and tests that can evaluate the resulting data. Nonetheless, researchers have been reexamining the basis of models and constructs used in management information systems, such as the stage hypothesis, and the resulting experiential data will be useful in developing the new insights needed to cope with the implementation of technology in this new information environment (Benbasat and others, 1984; King and Kraemer, 1984).

Figure 1 suggests an instrument for gathering data. It would be valuable to know whether the tasks that define the three roles model the experience of practitioners sufficiently well to make such frameworks useful. Practitioners could be asked to indicate how much time they spend on activities related to each task, how important each task has been in the past, how important it is now, and how important it is likely to be in the future. Thus, the related-roles diagram could become the basis for an instrument that could be used to gather field data that would help us to understand the important functional variables and thus to anticipate the consequences of changes in information technology.

Summation

This chapter speculates on the challenges and opportunities presented to institutional research by short-term changes in information technology, that is, by changes through the end of this decade. We begin by noting what technologies are changing. Next, we survey what can be said about approaches to impact analysis, about the nature of the underlying science and engineering that yields hints on the rates of future change, and about how we can manage the waves of new technologies as they play out their cycles in human organizations. We point to things that do not change, such as institutional culture and how campuses make decisions. The primary conclusion of this top-down analysis is that we ought to consider telematics a future speciality of institutional research.

The complementary bottom-up analysis identifies eighteen tasks or activities that together comprise three decision roles: decision maker, decision support intermediary, and telematics technologist. Interaction among these roles models a framework that describes institutional research functions in sufficient detail that we can begin to relate aspects of changing information technology to specific institutional research activities and hence to synthesize another set of speculations. This bottom-up analysis identifies major effects on the telematics technologist and suggests that including this role amounts organizationally for institutional research to assuming the functions of a campus information center and perhaps more responsibility for decision management.

Finally, both analyses underscore the need for finding better ways of recognizing, understanding, and evaluating change agents and of anticipating their consequences for higher education.

References

Benbasat, I., Dexter, A., Drury, D., and Goldstein, R. "A Critique of the Stage Hypothesis: Theory and Empirical Evidence." *Communications of the ACM,* 1984, *27* (5), 476-485.

Brown, K., and Droegemueller, L. "Microcomputer Use in Administrative Decision Support Systems." *Cause/Effect,* 1983, *6* (4), 12-19.

Canning, R. G. (Ed.). "The Changing Computing Environment." *EDP Analyzer,* 1984, *22* (9), 1-16.

Cash, J. I., Jr., McFarlane, F. W., and McKenney, J. L. *Corporate Information Systems Management.* Homewood, Ill.: Irwin, 1983.

Friedman, C. P. "Factors Affecting Adoption of Instructional Innovations: An Example from Medical Education." *Research in Higher Education,* 1982, *16* (4), 291-302.

Gerola, H., and Gomory, R. E. "Computers in Science and Technology: Early Indications." *Science,* 1984, *225* (257), 11-18.

Guimaraes, T. "The Evolution of the Information Center." *Datamation,* July 15, 1984, pp. 127-130.

Hackman, J. "The Seven Maxims for Institutional Researchers: Applying Cognitive Theory in Research." *Research in Higher Education,* 1983, *18,* 195-208.

Hample, S. "The Impact of Information Technology: Will IR Survive?" Paper issued by the Office of Institutional Research, Montana State University, April 1983.

Hayes-Roth, F., Waterman, D. A., and Lenat, D. B. (Eds.). *Building Expert Systems.* Reading, Mass.: Addison-Wesley, 1983.

Huber, G. P. "The Nature and Design of Postindustrial Organizations." *Management Science,* 1984, *30* (8), 928-951.

Huff, S. L., and Rivard, S. "The Amateur Data Processor: A New Organizational Role." *Business Quarterly,* 1983, *48* (4), 125-131.

Isenberg, D. J. "How Senior Managers Think." *Harvard Business Review,* 1984, *62* (6), 81-90.

Jedamus, P. "The Case for Decision Support Management." In W. Tetlow (Ed.), *Using Microcomputers for Planning and Management Support.* New Directions for Institutional Research, no. 44. San Francisco: Jossey-Bass, 1984.

King, J. L. "Centralized Versus Decentralized Computing: Organizational Considerations and Management Options." *Computing Surveys,* 1983, *15* (4), 319-349.

King, J. L., and Kraemer, K. L. "Evolution and Organizational Information Systems: An Assessment of Nolan's Stage Model." *Communications of the ACM,* 1984, *27* (5), 446-475.

Kuhns, E., and Martorana, S. V. (Eds.). *Qualitative Methods for Institutional Research.* New Directions for Institutional Research, no. 34. San Francisco: Jossey-Bass, 1982.

McCredie, J. W. (Ed.). *Campus Computing Strategies.* Bedford, Mass.: Digital Press, 1983.

Martin, J. *Design and Strategy for Distributed Data Processing.* Englewood Cliffs, N.J.: Prentice-Hall, 1981.

Mason, R. O., and Mitroff, I. I. *Challenging Strategic Planning Assumptions.* New York: Wiley, 1981.

Morrison, J. L., Renfro, W. L., and Boucher, W. I. (Eds.). *Applying Methods and Techniques of Futures Research.* New Directions for Institutional Research, no. 39. San Francisco: Jossey-Bass, 1983.

Nolan, R. L. *Managing the Data Resource Function.* St. Paul: West, 1982.

Norris, D. M., and Mims, R. S. "A New Maturity for Institutional Planning and Information Systems." *Journal of Higher Education,* 1984, *55* (6), 700-718.

Paschke, B. P., Nickolas, C. H., and Haren, T. "Planning Microcomputer Information Services: The Institutional Role." Paper presented at the 24th annual forum of the Association for Institutional Research, Fort Worth, May 6-9, 1984.

Pool, I. de S. (Ed.). *The Social Impact of the Telephone.* Cambridge, Mass.: M.I.T. Press, 1977.

Schmidtlein, F. A. "Decision Paradigms in Education." *Educational Researcher,* 1974, *3* (5), 4-11.

Sheehan, B. S. (Ed.). *Information Technology: Innovations and Applications.* New Directions for Institutional Research, no. 35. San Francisco: Jossey-Bass, 1982.

Sheehan, B. S. "Measurement for Decision Support." *Research in Higher Education,* 1984, *20,* 193-210.

Sholtys, P. "Systems Prototyping with Fourth-Generation Tools: One Answer to the Productivity Puzzle?" Paper presented at the 23rd annual forum of the Association for Institutional Research, Toronto, May 23-28, 1983.

Staman, E. M. (Ed.). *Examining New Trends in Administrative Computing.* New Directions for Institutional Research, no. 22. San Francisco: Jossey-Bass, 1979.

Stevenson, M., and Walleri, R. D. "Institutional Research and End User Computing: The Development of an Information Center." Paper presented at the 23rd annual forum of the Association for Institutional Research, Toronto, May 23-28, 1983.

Stevenson, M., and Walleri, R. D. "The Transformation of Institutional Research as a Result of Improving Technology." Paper presented at the 24th annual forum of the Association for Institutional Research, Fort Worth, May 6-9, 1984.

Bernard S. Sheehan is professor of management at the University of Calgary. He is a past president of the Association for Institutional Research.

The current state of the field and the impact of new environmental forces have substantial implications for the practice and profession of institutional research. They suggest that attention needs be given to the development of the profession, not just to the professional development of its members, and that the AIR needs a proactive, transformational leadership strategy.

Proliferation or Professional Integration: Transition or Transformation

Marvin W. Peterson
Mary Corcoran

This chapter asks three basic questions: First, what is the current state of institutional research? Second, what are the implications for institutional research of the current environmental changes? Third, what needs to be done if institutional research is to continue to be a viable institutional function that improves the performance of institutions of higher education?

The State of the Field

The current state of institutional research is perhaps best summarized as Cameron Fincher does in Chapter Two: It is a practicing art with commendable promise as a professional and technical specialty. However, as Peterson suggests in Chapter One, the field is currently subject to increasing fragmentation and uncertainty about its future direction.

As a field of practice, institutional research, despite some minor dissent, has evolved into a primarily management-oriented, applied, data-handling, analysis, and research function. The increased complexity of our institutions and systems, the increased accessiblity of data, and the increased availability of analytic capability in many administrative offices have led over the past five years to considerable dispersion and fragmentation of institutional research activity on many campuses. This development can be contrasted with the full decade of movement toward more coordinated or consolidated office structures that preceded it. Recent institutional pressures for reduction have increased the political pressure on institutional research and encouraged interest in a political, advocacy-oriented stance to research as units seek to defend their own resources, and the renewed institutional interest in planning has focused attention on policy research that is sometimes conducted elsewhere than in traditional institutional research offices. Finally, the growth of institutional research and the increasing diversity of its members have led to a proliferation and fragmentation of state and regional and special-interest groups within the AIR itself.

The wide array of activities and responsibilities that have been associated with institutional research (data collection, information system design, administrative computer specialists, external studies, resource and reduction analysis), the often extensive list of types of studies, the diverse methodologies used and data sources tapped, have all heightened the uncertainty about what constitutes institutional research.

It is not surprising, then, that a major concern for institutional researchers as the members of a profession is how to deal with the varied and often specialized interests of individuals who represent different academic backgrounds and work in an increasingly diverse array of institutions, agencies, and administrative offices. Concern for professional development (to keep abreast of an expanding field) and for personal advancement (where does this lead?) are central for many in the field.

As Cameron Fincher concludes, this highly interdisciplinary professional area lacks an integrative nexus of ideas or theories. Institutional research is an applied research field with a considerable repertory of methods, but it has as yet paid little attention to how well its array of methods serves higher education. There is a massive amount of data and information about institutions and institutional research practice, but there has been little synthesis of what we know or think is essential and most useful. Despite its scientific shortcomings, Fincher notes that practitioners in the field appreciate theory and practice and that they are concerned about the relevance and usefulness of their work and about enhancing their analytic and interpretive skills. With standards and norms of the field still emerging, practitioners need guidance in preparing for and entering the field and leadership in planning their professional development.

The AIR has grown with the practice and the profession. It has succeeded by growing and becoming more inclusive so as to accommodate new practitioners. In doing so, it has expanded its programs, its publications, and its membership subgroups to respond to the increasingly diverse interests of its members. Over time, it has added activities that broaden its functions. It began as a way of helping members to meet peers and share ideas (the early forums). Its functions broadened to include publications that captured new developments in the field and provided an outlet for member's work and activities that assisted members in keeping abreast and that furthered their professional development. The association's current concern about mission and direction reflects a sensitivity to the uncertainty and fragmentation that we have just invoked.

Impacts of the New Environment

The analyses contained in Chapters Three, Four, and Five suggest very different and contrasting pictures of the future of postsecondary education. These pictures have significant implications for institutional research. Table 1 depicts these implications.

Educational Environment. In Chapter Three, Heydinger portrays an educational reality in which fundamental shifts in the external environment may be occurring in demographic patterns, the basic values of youth, attitudes toward postsecondary education, costs of postsecondary education, retraining needs, patterns of educational competition and collaboration, the role of government, and communication technology. These changes suggest potentially extensive changes in the nature of postsecondary education and underscore the importance of examining educational futures. The primary roles of institutional research in this environment are those of educational and organizational future strategist and planner. Institutional research can play a critical role in providing research and analysis that assists in the formulation of comprehensive institutional and educational strategy. Such activity may be either centralized or carefully coordinated by a planning officer or function. It requires practitioners with a broad perspective, and it involves studying external environments, forecasting, assessing values and preferences, identifying internal strengths, creating scenarios, and assessing alternatives.

This perspective suggests a professional focus on educational and societal environments and on organization environment theories. The methodologies are both qualitative and quantitative and involve highly interdisciplinary modes of futures and planning research and policy analysis. Such research also relies heavily on the use of data bases from sources outside the institution and outside higher education. The emphasis is on broad educational and societal understanding, on ideas and enlightenment about possibilities and strategies, not on day-to-day operations or managerial responsibilities.

Governance and Management. In his views of governance and management, Schmidtlein shares some of Heydinger's and Sheehan's concerns. He sees management as being reshaped by the effects of external trends (particularly those causing institutional retrenchment) and by the rapid spread of microcomputer technology. He also is concerned about some emerging

Table 1. Implications of the New Environmental Reality

	Postsecondary Education	Governance	Telematics
The New Environmental Reality	Broad fundamental shifts External influences critical Needs and demands, delivery modes, institutional forms perhaps reshaped Importance of alternative futures	Limits of rationality Environmental evidence Complexity of resources Limits of the goal and problem concepts	Convergence of computing and communications Microcomputer development Information accessibility Decentralized analysis capacity
Implications for Practice			
1. Functions	Comprehensive, future educational strategist, institutional planner	Organizational integration, policy analyst, management analyst	Information expertise, telematics technologist, decision support intermediary
2. Structure	Centralized or coordinated with planning	Coordinated or dispersed	Centralized or coordinated
3. Content	Studies of environment, development of scenarios, assessment of alternatives	Studies of policy and managerial efficiency and effectiveness	Expertise in information and administrative computing systems, applications, and utilization
Implications for the Profession			
1. Science	Organization environment theory Quantitative and qualitative interdisciplinary methods Relevance of external data and sources	Organizational behavior, management science Quantitative and qualitative methods Information for decisions with rationale	Information, communication, and decision sciences Emphasis on quantitative methods Building of information networks
2. Art	Broad understanding of society and education Enlightenment, not operational	Comprehensive understanding of organization Systematic managerial perspective	Technological sophistication Information expertise

changes in the way we view the nature of organizations. His analysis identifies many of the issues that are attracting the attention of decision makers. He notes the increased reliance on data and information about external events, the importance of contextual factors in decision making, the increasingly broad range of resources to be considered when examining decision issues, the limitations of goals and problems as the focus of decision analysis, and the critical importance of the location of institutional research on its ability to influence decisions in a changing governance and management arena.

These observations suggest that the practice of institutional research will still be management oriented but that it will need to address these changing characteristics if it is to influence decisions effectively. The primary role or emphasis will be that of the policy analyst who informs broad planning and policy issues or of the management analyst who examines issues of institutional performance and complex decision issues. A major concern in times of tight resources is the improvement of organizational integration; institutional research needs to make this concern a criterion both of its research and of the organization of its own activities. Because management studies will continue to focus on efficiency and effectiveness in all areas of higher education, Schmidtlein sees a continued dispersal of institutional research and perhaps an increased need for coordination.

Schmidtlein's perspective rests on a theoretical view of organizational and administrative behavior and management science. The methodologies of these fields are probably not significantly different from the methodologies that institutional researchers employ; the emphasis on quality and on costs and benefits in planning, resource allocation, and evaluation suggests that both qualitative and quantitative methods are relied on. Also, while empirical studies are useful as information for decisions, they are likely to require extensive rationale and contextual or comparative data if they are to inform the difficult choices that must be made when resources are constrained. The perspective of professionals, he suggests, will be the perspective of individuals who have a comprehensive understanding of organizational or system dynamics and resources but whose orientation is to the concerns of management.

Telematics. In Chapter Five, Sheehan examines the convergence of computing and communications that is rapidly reshaping the information-handling and analysis capacity both of our institutions and of the field. The advent of microcomputers and the ease with which information can be stored and retrieved have already had one notable impact: decentralization of the capacity to do institutional studies to any office that has a microcomputer and access to institutional or other relevant data sets or the capacity to create its own. In Chapter One, Peterson noted that decentralization can fragment or politicize a college's institutional research capacity and undermine carefully integrated information systems and centralized or highly coordinated institutional research functions. In contrast, Sheehan suggests that decentralization can create two new role emphases or possibilities for institutional research: the telematics technologist or information center expert (chief information officer) who becomes the institution's expert on information-handling technology, and the decision support intermediary who serves decision makers. The first role suggests a centralized service function, while the second may involve coordination between decision makers and telematics technologists. In either role, the activities suggested by Sheehan's model involve either coordinating the development of information technology or applying it to decision support activities.

The professional implications of Sheehan's perspective suggest a strong conceptual base in information, communications, and decision science fields. The major emphasis is still on quantitative data and quantitative methods of analysis, although the techniques used for handling qualitative measures are expanding. One significant potential of this development lies in its ability to build information networks among institutional researchers that can enhance the exchange and synthesis of empirical findings. This area also suggests the potential merger of the art and science of this aspect of the profession, since the methodological sophistication is embedded in technology, and the standards (if not norms) are often dictated by the expertise required.

Contrasts and Common Themes. The relative importance of the three environments, the validity of the descriptions, and the analysis of their implications can be debated. The issue of primary concern for the development of institutional research as a field is the commonalities and differences among the three.

Clearly, the three environments suggest very different primary functions for the practice of institutional research: future strategist and institutional planner contrast with policy analyst and management analyst and with telematics technologist and decision support intermediary. As already noted, some environments suggest more centralized and others more coordinated or more dispersed structures, and the content or topics of analysis are highly varied.

The three environments suggest somewhat contrasting views of the science of institutional research. The concepts derive from societal perspectives, organizational environment theory, organizational and administrative behavior, management sciences, and information and communication sciences. The methodologies vary from the methods of interdisciplinary futurists, planning and forecasting, policy analysis, efficiency and effectiveness evaluations, organizational analysis, simulation and modeling, and information systems design to our traditional descriptive studies and reports. The empirical emphasis changes in each environment, but to varying degrees each environment includes quantitative and qualitative measures and methods; relies on internal data, external data, or both; and emphasizes both the use of information and the building of information networks.

When institutional research is viewed as an art, the three environments differ also in their levels of focus or analysis—societal, organizational, and technological—and in their sources of standards or norms—enlightened societal interest (values), management (process), and technical expertise (technology). Clearly, these contrasts do nothing to diminish current concerns about fragmentation in the field and uncertainty about the direction that it will take.

However, three common themes also emerge across the three environmental perspectives: First, although each new environmental reality implies different practical functions for institutional research, each new reality also stresses the importance of good information, analysis, and research in the future for viable educational strategy in a changing environment, for sound management in periods of constraint, and for effective use of the rapidly changing telematics technology. Second, despite their quite different theoretical or conceptual emphases, each perspective seems to recognize the importance of relating its theory, methods, and empirical approaches to the unique nature of postsecondary education. Third, all three perspectives suggest the need for some sophistication in relating theory and practice and for broad guides (if not standards) for good practice.

Proliferation or Professional Integration: Transition or Transformation?

The current tendency toward fragmentation in institutional research and uncertainty about future directions in practice, the profession, and the association was suggested by Peterson. The potential limitations of institutional research as a professional field were discussed by Fincher. The potential for further fragmentation posed by the three key environmental forces was analyed by Heydinger, Schmidtlein, and Sheehan, and it has been summarized here. The AIR's history of responding to members' concerns and of supporting professional development of the field has been discussed. Yet, the overwhelming evidence suggests that, if institutional research continues to evolve in its present pattern, proliferation and fragmentation are likely to continue. A heightened sense of professional direction and integration seems especially important in the years ahead.

The AIR's strategy has largely been reactive. It responds rapidly to new developments in the field and to new needs among its members. To date, this transitional strategy—assisting members to make transitions or adjustments to new developments—has been successful. One approach would be to continue this evolutionary or responsive transitional strategy. The AIR can seek out and incorporate as members practitioners who play the roles suggested by the three discussions of the environment in this volume. It can modify and expand its programs and publications so as to incorporate these new topics and interests (it already has to some extent), and it can plan professional development activities for the association that anticipate the interests of others in topics related to these developments.

Dealing with the current issues of uncertainty and fragmentation posed by Peterson will be critical. Dealing with Fincher's concerns about the need for development of the art and science of the field may require the association to adopt a more active role, providing professional leadership in defining the integrative themes. However, the challenge does not end there. As Heydinger, Schmidtlein, and Sheehan suggest, other forces promise to reshape institutional research even more extensively. Can reactive or responsive transitional strategy accommodate that reshaping? Or, will it require a more proactive transformation strategy, one that provides leadership by defining the direction of the profession as well as by identifying integrative themes and that reshapes the way we view the field of institutional research?

Our analysis leads us to conclude that the current responsive transitional strategy may not be sufficient. Both the current and impending changes are moving so rapidly and in so many different directions that a more action-oriented agenda is appropriate. Such an agenda would call for seeking a new level of professional identification and integration.

An Agenda for Development of the Profession

The previous analysis argues that the AIR should pay as much attention to development of the profession of institutional research (its direction and substantive integration) in the years ahead as it has to the professional development of its members in the past and that it needs to achieve a balance between these two emphases. Achieving that balance will involve the agenda depicted in Table 2.

Recognizing a New Reality. Institutions of higher education—their clientele, their delivery modes, and their programs, not just the institutional research function, could be very different within five to ten years. Both the changes in the educational environment and the educational implications of the telematics revolution, which Sheehan does not discuss, suggest that this is possible. Institutional researchers need to consider this possibility to understand both the context in which they work and their role and work itself. Like other faculty and administrators, they need to become serious students of the changing nature of their institutions, not just of their own offices and related activities.

An Intermediary Role. Similarly, institutional researchers need to recognize the critical intermediary role that their function plays between the educational, governance or managerial, and information or telematics functions of their institution. The research and analysis function is constantly shaped by all three, and it must relate to all three even if it serves primarily only one of these functions.

Need for a Common View of Practice. For a profession to develop, its members need to have a common understanding of their field of practice, if not of their theoretical endeavors. After early debates about the nature and nomenclature of institutional research, the term *institutional research* sufficed during the 1970s as practice became consolidated and as it was identified on many campuses with an office of institutional research. Recently, an influx of

Table 2. An Agenda for Professional Development

Dimension	Agenda Item
The New Institutional Reality	New forms of higher education possible
	Concern with their changing nature
	Institutional research in critical intermediary role
Institutional Research in Practice	Need for common view: institutional improvement
Function	Information collection, analysis, research, and utilization
	Related to planning, management, resource allocation, and evaluation
Structure	A process, not an office per se
Influence	Comprehensive strategies and methods
	More substantive knowledge (not information access and control)
Content	Varied studies and methods
Institutional Research as Profession	
Common Theme	Improvement of higher education
	Relating theory to practice
	Applied professional field
	Responsiveness to new roles and methods
Conceptual Base	Integrated interdisciplinary framework
Methodological Focus	Assessment of useful methods and techniques
Empirical Findings	Development of a substantive and methodological knowledge base
Sophistication	Relating of theory and practice
Standards and Norms	Examination of current patterns and needs
Other Developments	Telematics: development of information sharing and communication links
	Expansion of relationships with other researchers and administrative change leaders

members not affiliated with such offices and changes in the name or location of many such offices on college campuses have renewed the debates about the meaning of the term. For a profession—even an applied profession—a commonly accepted view of practice is required. Without proposing a new name, it does seem appropriate to conceive of the practice of institutional research as encompassing the following: an institutional process (not structure or office) that includes the collection or development of information, analysis of research, and utilization activities designed to improve some aspect of an institution of postsecondary education. Under this conception, institutional research includes varying types of research designed to serve planning, policy development, resource allocation, and management or evaluation decisions in all functional areas.

The intent of this definition is to include the different models or functions of institutional research, the varied organizational arrangements for institutional research functions, and the diverse methods that are employed. It places the focus on applied research that is concerned with improving the institution, not just with improving planning, resource management, resource allocation, or evaluation. We may have lost sight of the fact that improving the institution and its educational, research, and service function (not just its management functions and processes) is or should be our primary focus. In particular, the emphasis of this definition is on the process of institutional research, not on the structure of institutional research offices. Institutional research can be conducted in offices with different names or by individuals with different titles.

Shifting Bases for Influence. An applied activity like institutional research is supported only to the extent that it deals with critical institutional issues, that it is designed to help the institution function more effectively, and that it is credible. The chapters of this volume have suggested some important arenas for institutional research activity. Another implication is that the basis for influencing decisions may also be changing. During the 1960s and 1970s, one major source of an institutional researcher's influence and power was his or her access to and knowledge or control of institutional data. The advent of well-designed information systems and the spread of microcomputers removes to some extent this basis for influence. Skill in research methods and techniques, especially those involving complex computer simulations and models, has also been dispersed as new easy-to-use microcomputer software has placed powerful analytic capability within the reach of administrators concerned about influencing decisions that affect their own unit. The advent of concern for futures-oriented strategic policy or planning studies that use external data sources often allows individuals with different analytic skills and knowledge of external data sources to gain influence. In essence, these insights suggest that influence for institutional researchers is no longer as tied to knowledge and control of internal data or to sophisticated computer modeling skills as it once was; external sources and comprehensive research strategies that combine varied research methods and that use quantitative and qualitative data from internal and external sources are becoming increasingly important.

On another dimension, institutional researchers have often relied on research methods and techniques as their primary source of expertise. However, the role of substantive knowledge about postsecondary education may become more critical than methodological knowledge about institutional research methods and techniques. For example, executive officers considering a proposal for a new or alternative educational delivery mode may be more interested in knowing how effective it has been in attracting new students or in how it has affected learning. Answers to such questions should build on knowledge of the relevant research literature; both synthesis of existing studies and ad hoc institutional studies should be considered. Thus, access to other research findings and knowledge about substantive issues may be as critical in the future as good research design and methodological skills have been in the past.

A Common Professional Theme. For a profession to develop, it must have a common concern. One common view of the practice of institutional research has already been suggested. However, three elements appear to constitute the common bond for individuals participating in these various institutional research activities: First, they are concerned about institutional improvement in some specific area of institutional functioning, not about some kind of general improvement in management. Second, they share a concern for relating theory to practice. Institutional research is an applied field, yet the analysis of the three environments in this volume suggests that it is important to relate broad theoretical concepts to practice, and Fincher suggests that institutional researchers are aware of this need. Third, they identify institutional research as an applied professional field.

Responsiveness to New Roles and Methods. The history of institutional research suggests that the important institutional problems are constantly changing. If that is so, institutional research must use its data collection, analysis, and utilization skills to attack new problems or serve new needs and to continue to play new roles and adopt new methods as appropriate. The three environments examined in this volume suggest the need for new roles and methods such as these. It is important for a developing profession not to lose sight of this important characteristic of the field.

An Integrative Framework. The concern for understanding the new reality of changing educational conditions; the fragmenting pressures exerted by the diverse functions, theoretical underpinnings, and methods identified in both the description of the evolution of institutional research and in the analysis of the three environments; and Fincher's analysis of the awareness of the need for a nexus of ideas all underscore the timeliness and importance of developing an integrative framework from which we can view institutional research. Such a framework might have the following characteristics: It views colleges and universities as complex human organizations that include students, faculty, administrators, and staff. It views education from an open systems framework that recognizes environmental forces and influences. It pays attention to the distinctive characteristics of institutions of postsecondary education, their primary functions, and how they operate. It links resources with primary educational, scholarly, and service outputs. It focuses on understanding and informing the primary planning, management, resource allocation, and evaluation decisions. And, it includes appropriate internal and external data and information flows. Such a framework would of necessity be extensive and interdisciplinary, but it would reflect the arena of institutional research activity in postsecondary education.

Useful Methodologies. The preceding discussions all highlight the extensive array of inquiry methods used in institutional research and underscore the continual need to develop or borrow others. However, as Fincher notes, we often borrow and use methods and techniques that do not seem to be very useful. (PPBS always comes to mind.) To develop as a field, institutional research must continue to recognize the validity of diverse methods of inquiry (including both qualitative and quantitative methods), but we also need to begin to assess which methods and techniques are useful, which are not, and which might better serve higher education if they were modified. Currently, this process proceeds largely by trial and error, and there is no attempt to systematically review and assess new inquiry methods and techniques used in practice.

The Knowledge Base. As Fincher notes, institutional research has generated masses of data and studies, but we know little about the patterns of findings or about the appropriate substantive and methodological knowledge that it might be useful for an institutional researcher to possess. Before the field proliferates further, such syntheses would be useful, particularly if they were associated with an integrative framework and with the assessment of methodologies that proved useful in the past.

Sophistication, Standards, and Norms. While conceptual and methodological sophistication varies in an applied field of practice, institutional research should probably focus on increasing our sophistication in relating theory to practice. Only in that way is the level of discourse on development of the field likely to improve. Although discussion of standards and norms of good practice has some proponents, it seems likely to occur much later in the development of institutional research.

Information Sharing and Communication Links. The discussion of educational and governance environments highlighted the need for external and comparative data that reinforce earlier data exchange interests. Fincher notes that there are few syntheses of relevant findings and few assessments of which methods work and which do not. The advent of telematics makes interinstitutional data sharing and cross institutional identification of studies of similar issues much more feasible and with them the synthesis of findings and the assessment of different methodological techniques. Developments in this area could help individual practitioners in their work and the profession in its synthesis of findings and assessment of methods.

An Old Dialogue. The distinction between institutional research, which focuses on applied findings in a particular setting, and higher education research, which focuses on general patterns and theoretical interests, has been largely dormant since the early AIR forums. The proponents of each emphasis have largely gone their own way. Researchers in higher education now primarily attend Association for the Study of Higher Education or American Educational Research Association Division J meetings. However, this analysis suggests that the two may again have reasons to renew their dialogue. Clearly, the professional concerns for establishing an integrative framework and for conducting research on the effectiveness of various modes of inquiry (methods and techniques) are agenda items that might appeal to researchers in higher education. Similarly, institutional researchers who have interests in comparative research for planning and evaluation studies and who have an increasing need for substantive as well as methodological research findings may find that their interests are now more in line with those of their counterparts in higher education research. Further, the increasing sophistication of research methods, the interest in relating theory to practice, and the three critical environmental changes are all topics of interest to higher education researchers. Improved dialogue could prove a mutual advantage.

An Association Role: Reactive or Proactive, Transition or Transformation?

As noted earlier, the AIR can help both the field and the profession to evolve and develop by adopting a transitional role: by reacting supportively and responsively to the new functions, to potential members, and to the needs identified in the analysis of the three changing environments. These aims can be accomplished by incorporating these interests into existing meetings, publications, and professional development activities. However, such an approach may not succeed with the current proliferation of changes and forces.

An alternative agenda involves seeking a new level of development for the profession. This requires a proactive leadership role in which the association seeks to transform the way in which the profession views itself, its direction, and its role. Such a transforming role requires the association to address a more difficult agenda that addresses such questions as these: How do we develop knowledge about an entire field? How do we define its substance? How does an association lead rather than respond to its members? A modest action agenda based on the professional agenda sketched in Table 2 would include the following:

1. Give greater attention to the changing environment of postsecondary education and to the institutional context for institutional research.

2. Focus attention on the need for a common view of the practice of institutional research as an inclusive process of information collection, analysis, research, and utilization related to planning, management, resource allocation, and evaluation decisions. (This issue is singled out for attention in AIR's 1984 revised mission statement.)

3. Promote a professional theme focused on the improvement of institutions of postsecondary education through institutional research that relates theory to practice and that responds to new rational methods.

4. Take steps to develop an integrative framework for the field. There is none now. One could be prepared for the AIR's twenty-fifth anniversary.

5. Promote research activities and syntheses aimed at assessing the usefulness of methods and techniques. Current activities primarily identify and describe them.

6. Develop a knowledge base appropriate for the institutional research practitioner. Such a base would include substantive knowledge about postsecondary education, knowledge of important research methods and techniques, and information about important data and information sources. Such information probably exists, but synthesis and judgment about its importance are required.

7. Continue to stress relating institutional studies to theory or broader patterns of findings.

8. Assess current norms and standards of good practice among members.

9. Focus some current publication activities on systematic synthesis of useful methods, development of the knowledge base, and discussion of standards and norms of practice.

10. Make professional development activities more proactive by identifying new cutting edge areas for exploration. Continue to revise the annual AIR forum program and regional programs to reflect emerging interests and needs.

11. Actively promote membership among groups doing institutional research who do not have such titles.

12. Seek a more active involvement of and dialogue with education researchers and with administrative leaders interested in changing and improving institutions of postsecondary education.

13. Develop telecommunications and computerized information-sharing networks to serve members' professional and institutional needs more effectively.

It can be hoped that this agenda for the future will help to balance concern for the development of the profession with concern for the professional development of AIR members. It will limit the tendency toward proliferation, and we can hope that it will also assure that institutional research continues to be a major factor in the improvement of postsecondary education over the next twenty-five years.

Marvin W. Peterson is director of the Center for the Study of Higher Education at the University of Michigan. He is now president of the Association for Institutional Research.

Mary Corcoran is professor of higher education and educational psychology at the University of Minnesota. She is a former editor of AIR forum publications and a Distinguished Member of the association.

Index

A

Adams, C. R., 23, 37
American Council on Education (ACE), 6, 9; and Cooperative Institutional Research Program, 20, 29; Office of Statistical Information and Research of, 18
American Educational Research Association, 21, 111
Association: concept of, 2; evolution of, 6-13; role for, 111-112
Association for the Study of Higher Education, 111
Association of Institutional Research (AIR): European members of, 12, 29; evolution of, 5, 10, 11, 12, 13, 14, 100-101; forums of, 1, 6, 9, 11, 21, 29, 30, 69, 110; groups in, 100; as professional society, 2, 18, 21, 25, 32, 35; and transition or transformation, 105-106, 111-112
Astin, A., 42
Attitudes, impact of, 41-42

B

Benbasat, I., 95, 96
Blau, P. M., 71, 78
Boucher, W. I., 57, 97
Bowen, H. R., 26, 35
Bremner, J. E., 43, 57
Breneman, D., 62, 78
Brooks, G. E., 9, 15
Brown, K., 81n, 85, 96
Brumbaugh, A. J., 5, 14, 18, 26, 28, 34, 35
Budgets, justifications for, 66-67

C

California, minority youth in, 41
California at Los Angeles, University of, and Cooperative Institutional Research program, 42
CAMPUS (Comprehensive Analytical Methods for Planning in University/College Systems), 24
Canning, R. G., 88, 96
Cash, J. I., Jr., 84, 96
Chulak, J., 11
Cohen, M. D., 75, 78
Coleman, J. S., 25, 36
College and University Environment Scales (CUES), 22
Colorado, flexibility in, 65
Competition, impact of, 44, 50-51
Computer modeling, as model, 24-25
Control Data Corporation, competition from, 44
Cooperative Institutional Research Program (CIRP), 20, 29, 42
Corcoran, M., 1-4, 99-112
Costs: administrative, concerns with, 67; of education, impact of, 42-43
Cowley, W. H., 5, 6, 14
Crenson, M. A., 36
Crissey, B. L., 36
Cronbach, L. J., 22, 36

D

Data processing, basics of, 86
Decisions: institutional processes for, 87; location shifts for, 63-64; support, and telematics, 81-97
Demography, impact of, 40-41
Development function, growth of, 64
Dexter, A., 96
Doi, J. I., 5, 6, 14
Dressel, P. L., 30, 36
Droegemueller, L., 85, 96
Drury, D., 96
Dyer, H. S., 18-19, 22, 28, 34, 36
Dyer, T. G., 17, 36

E

Educational research model, 21-22
Educational Testing Service, 19
Environmental scanning technique, 52-53
Equal Educational Opportunity Study, 25
Equity, impact of concern with, 68-69
Evaluation research model, 23-24

113

F

Faculty: attractiveness of careers for, 45; vitality of, 64-65
Financial aid, impact of, 67-68
Fincher, C., 3, 14, 17-37, 59, 99, 100, 105, 109, 110
Florida State University, association national office at, 11
FOCUS, 85
Foresight Task Force, 53, 54, 57
Friedman, C. P., 83, 96

G

Gallup, G. W., 41, 57
General Electric, and strategic planning, 63
Georgiou, P., 73, 78
Gerola, H., 84, 96
Gerth, H. H., 61, 78
Gideonse, H. D., 22, 36
Glenny, L. A., 11, 15, 20, 36, 62, 78
Goldstein, R., 96
Gomory, R. E., 84, 96
Governance and management: analysis of changing strategies for, 59-79; conclusions on, 78; and external trends, 60, 62-69; implications of, 101-103; and organizational character, 61-62, 69-77; and retrenchment, 62-67; sources of change for, 59-62; and technological change, 60-61
Government regulation, impact of, 46
Gray, J., 18, 36
Greenberger, M., 24, 36
Gross, F. M., 25, 36
Guimaraes, T., 93, 96

H

Hackman, J., 92, 96
Hample, S., 81n, 93, 96
Haren, T., 97
Hawken, P., 47n, 48, 55, 57
Hayes-Roth, F., 85, 96
Hearn, J. C., 52, 57
HELP/PLANTRAN (Higher Education Long-Range Planning/Planning Translator), 24
Heydinger, R. B., 3, 39-47, 60, 62, 63, 101, 105, 106
Higher education: adaptations possible for, 46-51; analysis of forces affecting future of, 39-57; environmental information for, 51-55; external forces on, 40-46; flexibility needs of, 65-66; implications of, 101, 102; institutional culture in, 85; official future for, 48; scenarios for, 48-51; sources of change for, 59-62
Higher Education General Information Survey (HEGIS), 29
Hodgkinson, H., 40, 41, 57
Homans, G., 71, 78
Hoos, I. R., 22, 36
Huber, G. P., 85, 96
Huff, S. L., 92, 96
Hyatt, J. A., 62, 78

I

I.B.M. Canada, and information center, 93
Ilchman, W. F., 71, 78
Information center (IC), growth of, 93-94
Information technology: analysis of developments in, 81-97; background on, 81-82; and change dimensions, 82-83; changes possible in, 87-88; changing factors in, 83-85; context and content for, 94-95; and governance and management, 60-61; impact analysis framework for, 82-83, 88-89, 91-92; impact of, 44-45; and institutional research functions, 88-92; and organization of institutional research, 93-94; persistent features of, 85-87; and research possibilities, 95
Institutional Functioning Inventory (IFI), 22
Institutional Goals Inventory (IGI), 22
Institutional research: analysis of, 17-37; as art, 30-34, 35; background on, 17-18; bases for influence of, 108-109; challenges for, 14; concept of, 107-108; context and content of, 94-95; contrasts and common themes in, 104-105; decision maker role in, 89-90; decision support intermediary role in, 90; developmental status of, 34-35; emergence of, 6, 9-10; empirical findings in, 29-30; 35, 107; and environmental information, 51-55;

evolution of, 5-15; fragmentation and uncertainty of, 12-13; functions changing in, 88-92, 107; and governance and management strategies, 59-79; greening of, 88; growth and consolidation of, 10-12; and higher education's future, 39-57; impacts of environment on, 101-105; institutional impact of, 32-34, 35; intermediary function of, 5; issues changing in, 19-20; methods of inquiry in, 20, 28-29, 30-32, 35, 107, 109, 110; models influencing, 21-27; organization of, 93-94; organizational location of, 75-77; publications for, 11-12, 29; role interaction in, 90-91; as science, 27-30, 35; as science of institutions, 18-20; skills needed for, 55-57; standards and norms of, 32, 35, 107, 110; state of field of, 99-101; structures of, 88, 107; and telematics, 81-97; telematics specialty in, 88, 107; telematics technologist role in, 90, 93-94; theoretical bases for, 28, 35, 107, 110; transition or transformation of, 14, 99-112

Isenberg, D. J., 89, 96

Issues management technique, 52, 53-54

J

Jedamus, P., 30, 36, 81n, 93-94, 96
Jencks, C., 25, 36
Jossey-Bass, 11, 29

K

Kahn, R. L., 60, 61, 78
Kaiser Aluminum, and issues management, 54
Katz, D., 60, 61, 78
Keller, G., 62, 78
Keller Graduate School of Business, competition from, 44
Kellogg Foundation, W. K., 39n
Kentucky, flexibility in, 65
Kerr, C., 65, 79
King, J. L., 88, 95, 96
Kraemer, K. L., 95, 96
Kuhn, T. S., 61, 79
Kuhns, E., 88, 96

L

Lawrence, G. B., 29, 36
Lenat, D. B., 96
Litigation, impact of, 68-69

M

McCredie, J. W., 88, 97
McFarlane, F. W., 96
McKenney, J. L., 96
Management. *See* Governance and management
MAPPER, 85
March, J. G., 78
Martin, J., 83, 97
Martorana, S. V., 88, 96
Maryland, flexibility in, 65
Mason, R. O., 87, 97
Mason, T. R., 24, 36
Mayeske, G. A., 25, 36
Measured outcomes model, 25-26
Measurement and assessment model, 22
Meyer, T. J., 42, 57
Microcomputers, impact of, 69
Mills, C. W., 61, 78
Mims, R. S., 93, 97
Mingle, J. R., 25, 36, 62, 79
Minnesota: flexibility in, 65; population ages in, 41
Minnesota, University of: educational research at, 17-18; Experimental Team on External Assessment of, 52-53; scenarios for, 46, 48-51; tuition at, 42
Mitroff, I. I., 89, 97
Moore's law, and information technology, 83-84
Morrison, J. L., 52, 57, 82, 97
Multiple scenario analysis technique, 52, 54-55

N

National Center for Education Statistics, 29
National Center for Higher Education Management Systems (NCHEMS), 12, 29
National Commission on Excellence in Education, 53, 57

New England Board of Higher Education (NEBHE), 9
New Mexico, minority youth in, 41
Newsted, P., 81n
Nickolas, C. H., 97
Nolan, R. L., 84, 97
Norris, D. M., 93, 97
NPL, 85

O

Ogilvy, J., 57
Olsen, J. P., 78
Operations research model, 23
Organizations: character of, 61-62, 69-77; economic standards of, 71-72; goal sepcification by, 73-74; institutional research locations in, 75-77; issues as solvable problems for, 74-75; rationality of, 70-71

P

Paschke, B. P., 93, 97
Peters, T. J., 61, 65, 79
Peterson, M. W., 1-15, 36, 99-112
Pflaum, A., 39n
Planning: and environmental information, 50-55; as model, 25
PLATO, 44
Plourde, P. J., 25, 36
Policy Analysis, Incorporated, and issues management, 53
Policy research and analysis model, 26-27, 30-31
Pool, I. de S., 82, 97
Postsecondary education. See Higher education
Practice: concept of, 2; evolution of, 6-13
Profession: agenda for development of, 106-111; common view of, 106-108, 109; concept of, 2; evolution of, 6-13; information sharing and communication in, 110; integrative framework for, 109-110; intermediary role of, 106; new reality for, 106
Program budgeting model, 25

R

RAMIS, 85
Reaganism, 47

Redford, E. S., 75-76, 79
Reichard, D. J., 57
Renfro, W. L., 53, 57, 97
Retraining needs, impact of, 43-44, 49
Retrenchment: and external focus, 62-63; impact of, 62-67
Rivard, S., 92, 96
Rourke, F. E., 9, 15
RRPM (Resource Requirements Prediction Model), 24
Rudolph, F., 40, 57
Russell, J. D., 18

S

Sanford, N., 18, 19, 20, 36
Santiago, A. A., 78
Schietinger, E. F., 30, 36
Schmidtlein, F. A., 3, 59-79, 90, 97, 101, 103, 105, 106
Schomberg, S., 39n
Schroeder, T. G., 23, 37
Schulman, C. H., 78
Schwartz, P., 57
SEARCH (System for Evaluating Alternative Resource Commitments in Higher Education), 24
Service, A. L., 29, 36
Sheehan, B. S., 3, 44, 60-61, 69, 81-97, 101, 103-104, 105, 106
Shell Oil Company, interdisciplinary teams at, 56
Shirley, R. C., 62, 79
Sholtys, P., 85, 97
Society, interaction with segments of, 45-46
Society for College and University Planning (SCUP), 25
Software, changing, 85
Southern Regional Education Board (SREB), 9
SRI, and issues management, 53
Stages hypothesis, and information technology, 84
Staman, E. M., 93, 97
Stecklein, J., 10
Stevenson, M., 81n, 93, 97
Study Group on the Conditions of Excellence in American Higher Education, 67, 79
Suppes, P., 22, 36
Systems analysis model, 22-23

T

Technology. *See* Information technology
Telematics: analysis of, for decision support, 81-97; concept of, 84; implications of, 102, 103-104; in institutional research, 90; 93-94; specialty of, 88, 107
Tennessee, performance measures in, 66
Tetlow, W. L., 69, 79

U

Uphoff, N. T., 71, 78

V

Values, impact of, 42, 49-50
Vickers, G., 73-74, 79

W

Walleri, R. D., 93, 97
Wang Institute, competition from, 44
Waterman, D. A., 96
Waterman, R. H., Jr., 61, 65, 79
Weber, M., 61
Weick, K., 40, 57
West, E. D., 18
Western Interstate Commission on Higher Education, 9
Westinghouse, course catalogue of, 43
Wilensky, H. L., 26, 37
Wilson, I., 53

Z

Zentner, R., 47*n*, 48, 55, 57

Ministry of Education & Training
MET Library
13th Floor, Mowat Block, Queen's Park
Toronto   M7A 1L2